R. Hugel.

STRANGE TEXTS
BUT GRAND TRUTHS

STRANGE TEXTS
BUT
GRAND TRUTHS

CLARENCE E. MACARTNEY

ABINGDON-COKESBURY PRESS

NEW YORK   NASHVILLE

STRANGE TEXTS BUT GRAND TRUTHS

Library of Congress Catalog Card Number: 52-13756

SET UP, PRINTED, AND BOUND BY THE
PARTHENON PRESS, AT NASHVILLE,
TENNESSEE, UNITED STATES OF AMERICA

FOREWORD

Many great texts which strike the chord of cardinal Christian truth are neglected by the preacher. Their very familiarity tempts him to bypass them. But there are also many striking and unusual texts in the Bible, seldom, if ever, used, which give the preacher opportunity to express practical, important, timely, and timeless truths. The very fact that an unusual text arouses the curiosity of the hearer and causes him to wonder what can be made of such a text, what lesson for time and for eternity can be drawn from it, will certainly be no handicap to the preacher.

Clarence Edward Macartney

CONTENTS

"A woman slew him."
Judg. 9:54

A COMMON EPITAPH

AN OLD SAYING HAS IT, "COUNT NO MAN HAPPY UNTIL the end." This certainly was true in the case of Gideon. His bright day had set in darkness and in gloom. The hero of the grand victory over the host of the Midianites had fallen a victim to the glory of that victory. Out of the golden earrings, pendants, chains, wristlets, and anklets taken from the fallen foe, Gideon made an ephod which was worshiped by Israel as an idol. Thus the man who commenced his great career by hewing down the idols of Baal and overthrowing their altars concludes his history by leading Israel astray. And the ephod was set up, the sacred chronicler tells us, "even in Ophrah." Where was Ophrah? It was beneath the oak of Ophrah that Gideon was visited by the angel of the Lord. There he received the sign of the fleece which was wet with dew when the ground was dry; and there he built his altar to the Lord. "Even at Ophrah," the place of early consecration and devotion. That tells the story of many a man's decline and fall.

But whatever his mistakes toward the close of his life, Gideon at first did not succumb to the lure of fame and hero worship. When the people sought to crown him as king, he declined to accept the crown, saying that neither he nor his son should rule over them, but that the Lord was to be their king.

THE END OF ABIMELECH

When the funeral was over, the family quarrels commenced. Gideon had numerous sons by his wives and concubines. One of these sons, Abimelech, was a base man, contemptible, lawless, and hard; yet not without ambition. His being the son of a concubine shut him out from a chance for the throne, should Israel decide to have a king. Abimelech therefore went among his mother's friends at Shechem and persuaded them to assist him in the slaughter of the seventy sons of Gideon on one stone at Ophrah. Then "all the men of Shechem" went out to crown Abimelech king by the oak which was in Shechem.

But Abimelech's bloody knife had not completely finished its work. Jotham, the youngest son of Gideon, had escaped. That is always the way with evil and evil deeds—truth and righteousness are never left without an heir to the throne. Some youngest son escapes the sword and comes back to judge. Evil builds its tower, grim and strong-walled. But it leaves some chink or crevice through which at length the arrow of judgment finds its way. Just as the men of Shechem were crying out, "God save the king," Jotham appeared on a rocky crag above the town and pronounced his fable of the trees.

The trees went forth to anoint a king over them. They said to the olive tree, "Reign thou over us." But the olive tree answered, "Should I leave my fatness, wherewith by me they honor God and man, and go to wave to and fro over the trees?" Then the trees gave an invitation to the fig tree to reign over them. But the fig tree answered,

10

"Should I leave my sweetness, and my good fruit, and go to wave to and fro over the trees?" Then the trees asked the vine to reign over them. But the vine also declined the honor, saying, "Should I leave my new wine, which cheereth God and man, and go to wave to and fro over the trees?" As a last resort the assembly of the trees invited the bramble to be their king. The bramble accepted the honor but said, "If in truth ye anoint me king over you, then come and take refuge in my shade; and if not, let fire come out of the bramble, and devour the cedars of Lebanon."

As soon as he had delivered himself of this powerful parable, Jotham disappeared into the mountains. His prophecy quickly came true. The people had rejected and slain the sons of Gideon who might have ruled them with justice and equity, and had chosen Abimelech, the basest and wickedest of men, to be their king, even as the trees had chosen the bramble for a king. Now they must serve Abimelech with slavish fear, or he would burn them in his wrath. In three years the men of Shechem grew tired of their king and rebelled against him. Abimelech came with his army, took the city by storm, slew the people, beat down the walls, and sowed the place with salt. If any men of Shechem were left to tell the tale, they must have recalled the words of Jotham: "Let fire come out of the bramble, and devour the cedars of Lebanon."

But malcontents and rebels were still left in the town of Thebez. The energetic and capable Abimelech stormed the city, the defenders and all the inhabitants of which had shut themselves up in a strong tower. Abimelech and his men surrounded the tower and were about to set fire to it, as they had done to the tower of Shechem, when

11

a woman on the top of the tower hurled the upper part of a millstone down upon the assailants. The stone struck Abimelech and crushed his head. The dying warrior said to his armor-bearer, "Draw thy sword, and kill me, that men say not of me, A woman slew him." At that his armor-bearer drew his sword and gave Abimelech the finishing stroke.

The story of the death of Abimelech has its parallel in the death of the great soldier of antiquity, Pyrrhus. In the siege of Argos, Pyrrhus and his men suffered a repulse. They might have withdrawn in safety but for the ferocity and loyalty and sagacity of one of their own elephants. The driver of this elephant had been hurled from his back in the melee, and the loyal beast, trumpeting loudly for his friend and master, turned and charged through friend and foe in search of the missing driver. Finding him, the elephant picked him up with his trunk and then charged back through the soldiers of both armies, treading down friend and foe in his fury. Pyrrhus might have escaped, but in this confusion he returned to the battle. An enemy soldier smote him in the breast with a lance, and Pyrrhus was about to retaliate, when the soldier's mother, watching the battle from a parapet and seeing her son in jeopardy, hurled a piece of a tile from the roof down upon the head of Pyrrhus. Thus, like Abimelech of old, the great warrior met his death. "A woman slew him."

MEN WHOM WOMEN SLEW

Abimelech besought his armor-bearer to run him through with the sword so that his name might escape the shame and odium of the fact that "a woman slew him." That phrase, taken out of its military setting, is the epitaph which I read upon the grave of many an able and gifted man. That brief epitaph is a summary of the history of those whose lamp of talent has been put out, whose happiness has been clouded, whose influence has been destroyed, and whose lives have been darkened by association with the wrong kind of woman.

How that epitaph, "A woman slew him," sounds through the Bible with deep reverberation and solemn warning! Thus fell the first man. "The woman . . ., she gave me of the tree, and I did eat." Jacob, long after he had become a prince with God, sold himself to a harlot. Samson had the Spirit of God upon him and performed mighty exploits, only at length to sell in the lap of Delilah the secret of his strength and to end his days "eyeless in Gaza, at the mill with slaves."

David, the sweet singer of Israel, man of generous impulses, of noble magnanimity, the man after God's heart, suddenly plunges to abysmal depths of murder and treachery because of the fatal vision he had as he walked the roof garden of his palace on a summer evening. Solomon, builder of the temple of God, man of profound erudition and author of great sayings, chosen of God because in his youth he had chosen the wisdom of God rather than wealth or fame, in his old age succumbs to the lure of heathen women and bends his aged knees in the worship of strange gods. Ahab, through the taunts and influence of the wicked Jezebel, sheds the blood of innocent Naboth and persecutes the prophets of the Lord. Haman, chagrined over the fact that Mordecai does not do him honor, is persuaded by his wife to erect a gallows upon which Mordecai is to be hanged, but Haman himself meets his death there.

13

On the grave of each of these men, at least for one particular chapter of his life, the epitaph I read is this, "A woman slew him." This epitaph is pronounced not with any thought of condemning the woman more than the man, or exculpating these men from responsibility for their evil deeds and for their ruin, but only to show what power to wreck and to destroy there is in the association of men and women. This association can be strong for good; there is nothing stronger. But it can also be strong for evil, and there is nothing stronger. If on many a grave we can read the epitaph, "A woman slew him," so also on a multitude of graves we can read another epitaph, "A man slew her." But for the present we deal with only one side of this solemn and impressive truth.

I recall a man who once came in great distress to see me. A man of family, he had become involved in a sinful relationship which was leading him straight down to ruin and disaster. He himself realized that, else he would not have come to talk with me. When I pointed out to him the certain consequences of the course he was pursuing, and told him that the only safe and honorable thing for him to do was to break the relationship, he answered sadly and yet with the accent of finality, "I can't let her go!" What he said is an example of the terrible power and mysterious fascination of such a relationship. Even when he saw the handwriting on the wall, he felt himself incapable of decision and action.

A woman came to me some time ago, asking me if I could not do something to break the friendship which her husband had established with another woman. He had been a good husband; they had lived long and happily together and had seen their children grow to young man-

14

hood and young womanhood. He had been successful as a man of business. But now, under the terrible spell of this infatuation, he had deserted his family, lost the respect of his friends and associates, and suffered in business. It was an example of the total wreck of a life when once it strikes on the rock of such a sinful relationship.

One of the saddest and most striking instances of a gifted man slain by a woman was the fall of the gifted and brilliant Irish leader and patriot of the last quarter of the nineteenth century, Charles Stewart Parnell. Well-born and well-educated, and a Protestant, Parnell led the fight in Ireland and in the English Parliament for home rule and freedom in Ireland. He had the confidence and the enthusiastic backing of hundreds of thousands of Irishmen of all ranks. When he came to America, multitudes of Irish Americans and Irish sympathizers were captivated by his personality and his eloquence. Then, suddenly, like Lucifer, he fell from heaven. In 1889 his associate and fellow agitator, Captain O'Shea, brought civil action against Parnell for adultery with O'Shea's wife. Parnell made no defense. Afterward he married Mrs. O'Shea.

At first this tragic episode in his personal life seemed to have little effect upon Parnell's extraordinary popularity and influence with the people of Ireland. But soon it became apparent that he had committed political suicide. In a famous letter to John Morley, Prime Minister Gladstone declared that the Liberal party and the home rule supporters in Parliament would be compelled to dissociate themselves from Parnell and all his works, and that unless he were deposed as leader of the Irish party, the Liberals in Parliament would no longer advocate home rule. Parnell issued answers of defiance, claiming that his personal life had nothing to do with his political actions. But it was not so to be. When he married Mrs. O'Shea, the Irish Catholic bishops and archbishops repudiated him, and finally his own Irish party deposed him as their leader. Thus a great political career was wrecked. A woman slew him.

History affords no more striking and terrible illustration of how an infatuation for the wrong kind of woman can ruin even the greatest of men. When Mark Antony was at Tarsus, in Cilicia, where Paul was born, and was making preparations for the Parthian War, he sent a message to Cleopatra, the "serpent of the Nile," to make her appearance at Tarsus and answer the charge that she had assisted his enemy Cassius in the late wars. In his great chapter on Mark Antony, Plutarch says of this meeting between Antony and Cleopatra: "The last and crowning mischief that could befall him came in the love of Cleopatra, to awaken and kindle to fury passions that as yet lay still and dormant in his nature, and to stifle and finally corrupt any elements that yet made resistance in him of goodness and a sound judgment."

Cleopatra appeared at Tarsus, but she appeared as the conqueror she was going to be, instead of one who was to answer to a charge. She sailed up the river Cydnus in a gilded barge with sails of purple, whose oars of silver beat time to the music of flutes and fifes and harps, while she herself lay under a canopy of cloth of gold, dressed as Venus, with "beautiful young boys, like painted cupids," and her maids like sea nymphs standing about her. Plutarch says of Cleopatra, "Plato admits four sorts of flattery, but she had a thousand." To these charms and flatteries Antony swiftly succumbed, and his great ambitions and high opportunity were lost sight of in this unfortunate infatuation.

In the midst of the great naval battle of Actium, fought September 2, 31 B.C., between the fleet of Octavian, afterward Caesar Augustus, and the fleets of Cleopatra and Mark Antony, when the issues of the day were still undecided, the sixty ships of Cleopatra broke from the battle and fled; Antony, seeing that she was leaving the scene of battle, "showed to all the world that he was no longer actuated by the thoughts and motives of a commander or a man," and he proved the truth of the old jest that "the soul of a lover lives in someone else's body"; for as soon as he saw Cleopatra's ships departing, he abandoned all his ships and the thousands who were fighting and spending their lives for him and sailed after Cleopatra, "to follow her that had so well begun his ruin and would hereafter accomplish it."

The assassination of Sisera, the captain of the Canaanite army, by Jael, the wife of Heber, has long been the subject of debate and discussion. Whether it was an act of base treachery or, as Deborah in her great song makes it out to be, an inspired act of valor and patriotism which gives Jael a place among the heroines of Israel, is the question. But however that may be, the fact and the manner of the death of Sisera may well be used as a picture and illustration of the downfall of a man. When, after the rout of his army on the banks of the Kishon River, Sisera, a fugitive and alone, appeared near the encampment of the Kenites and seemed to be hesitating to enter and take refuge there, Jael came out to meet him; and, saluting him with great gracious courtesy, as if Sisera were a conqueror instead of a fugitive, she invited him into her

tent, saying, "Turn in, my lord, turn in to me; fear not."
When Sisera entered her tent and asked for a drink of
water, she gave him milk to drink instead; and when he
asked for food, she brought forth butter in a lordly dish;
and when he lay down upon the couch to rest, she covered
him with a goodly mantle. He had charged her before he
fell into his fatal sleep that if any pursuer came to ask if
there was a man in the tent, she was to say, No. Alas
for Sisera! His real peril was not from Barak, or any
other pursuer, but from the woman who gave him milk
to drink and brought him butter in a lordly dish. While
the exhausted Sisera lay in sleep, Jael stole into the tent,
holding in one hand a tent pin and in the other a hammer.
Kneeling down, she put the point of the tent pin against
his exposed temple, and then with her hammer struck
once, twice, and thrice. "At her feet he bowed, he fell, he
lay down: at her feet he bowed, he fell: where he bowed,
there he fell down dead."

The flattery of Jael when she brought Sisera butter in
a lordly dish deceived him. In a weak moment, a moment
of exhaustion and fear, he was slain. Instead of falling in
battle, he perished in a woman's tent, under the hammer
of Jael. Men are often slain in their sleep. They are slain
when their ambition is asleep; they are slain when their
honor is asleep; they are slain when their conscience is
asleep; they are slain when their religion is asleep.

"For Herodias' sake" is the epitaph placed by Mark
on the grave of Herod Antipas. John the Baptist had rebuked Herod and Herodias for their adulterous union.
For this reason "Herodias had a quarrel against him."
She would have killed him, but she could not. Instead of
killing John, as Herodias desired, Herod shut him up in

a prison. Mark says that "Herod feared John, knowing that he was a just man and an holy, . . . and when he heard him, he did many things, and heard him gladly." That means that Herod frequently brought John out of prison and had him preach to him. But the fatal day for John was Herod's birthday, when Salome, the daughter of Herodias, danced before Herod and his wine inflamed lords and nobles. Greatly pleased with her dance, Herod said to Salome, "Whatsoever thou shalt ask of me, I will give it thee, unto the half of my kingdom." Salome probably would have asked for a villa, or a costly necklace, or a chariot; but when she consulted her mother, the vindictive Herodias said to her, "Ask for the head of John the Baptist!" When he heard that terrible request, Herod was sorry; "yet for his oath's sake, and for their sakes which sat with him," but chiefly for Herodias' sake, he granted the request of Salome, and the head of John the Baptist was brought before him in a charger. Here is the tragedy of a man to whom the Spirit of God had been speaking, and who, when he heard John preach, responded to him and was on the way to a better life. But "for Herodias' sake" he slew him. A woman slew him!

I remember one of the tales that my mother used to tell her children. It was of an army officer in India who had a tiger cub for a pet. The cub was an affectionate and playful animal, and was often with its master. At length it had grown to size and strength. One day the officer was sitting in his library reading. As he read, he fell asleep. The young tiger, lying by his master's chair, began to lick the hand which hung down near him. There was a slight abrasion on the hand, and as the tiger licked the wound, he tasted blood. With the taste of blood he became more and more ardent, until the officer, awakening, found himself looking into the blazing yellow eyes, not of a playful tiger cub, but of a ferocious beast that had tasted his blood and now sought his life. Just in time, he seized his pistol and shot the tiger. That story left a great impression upon me; and, so far as its figurative meaning in the realm of morals and temptation is concerned, experience with life has only served to confirm that early impression. The wrong relationship which today seems only pleasant and delightful, tomorrow may be the tiger thirsting for your blood.

This is not written just for the sake of stating and illustrating a solemn and alarming fact of life. It is meant as a warning; it is meant as an invitation; it is meant as an appeal; it is meant for the welfare of some immortal soul. Are you in a situation comparable to that of any one of those men of whom I have spoken in this sermon? Is your conscience dimmed by the mist of indulgence? Is your ambition asleep? Is your honor asleep? Is your religion asleep? Are you looking only at the things that are near and temporal, and forgetting the things which are unseen and eternal? Are you asleep to the welfare of your soul, to the great issues of time and eternity? Then, "Awake thou that sleepest, and arise from the dead, and Christ shall give thee light."

II

"Alas, master! for
it was borrowed."
II Kings 6:5

ALAS! FOR IT WAS BORROWED

THE STORY OF ELISHA GIVES THE FIRST MENTION IN
history of a school or college of any kind. It was a school
of the prophets, where they studied the queen of sciences,
the science of God, theology.

It takes more than timber, or brick, or stone, to make
a college, or a school of the prophets. President James A.
Garfield was a graduate of Williams College. At a meeting once of the alumni of New York he said that his idea
of the equipment and endowment of a college was a log
in the woods with a student and a book at one end and
Mark Hopkins, the celebrated Williams president, at the
other.

On the banks of the Neshaminy Creek, some twenty
miles out from Philadelphia, there is a memorial stone
which marks the site of the "Log College" founded by
William Tennent. The inscription on the stone tells you
that out of the Log College, established early in the eighteenth century, came fifty and more colleges, commencing
with Princeton. The great soul hunter, George Whitefield,
visited this school of the prophets and said it made him
think of the school of the prophets over which Elisha pre-

sided. It was a rude log building, but it had a great teacher, William Tennent.

On the banks of Service Creek, on the south side of Beaver County, there is a monument marking the site and the home of a Scottish, Edinburgh-trained minister who there gathered together a few young men and trained them in the languages of the Scriptures and in divinity. It was just a crude wilderness building, but it had a great teacher, John Anderson. The school that he taught there, still existing today under the name of the Pittsburgh-Xenia Theological Seminary, is the third oldest in America.

On what used to be the campus of Jefferson College at Canonsburg, Pennsylvania, stands a small log building with great memories. It was the Log Academy which stood near the home of John McMillan, not far from the Hill Church, and where he gathered together young men and trained them for the ministry. It was just a little log hut, and yet out of it came influences which are felt in western Pennsylvania to this day.

Yes; it takes more than brick and stone and timber to make a college or a seminary. If someone were to give me ten million dollars, to be given to some college or colleges, I would not spend it in buildings. I would use it to endow chairs for teachers and professors of the highest ability who would be able to train young men for the future and to build that kind of character which the church and the nation so sorely need today.

In spite of the low state of religion at that time in Israel, the school of the prophets prospered until the dormitory the students occupied was too strait, too limited, for the accommodation of the students. When Elisha came to give them one of his lectures, they asked permission of him to build a larger seminary. Elisha gladly gave his consent. There was no church extension committee then to help them, but each student went to work with a hearty will. Along the banks of the Jordan the trees were more plentiful than in any other part of Palestine. That is true today. The students, with Elisha accompanying them, went down to the Jordan and into the forest along its banks, armed with axes. Laying aside their prophetic and academic robes, they fell to with their axes. The forest echoed with their shouts of mutual encouragement, and there was the stirring music of the thud of the ax and the crash of falling trees.

One of the young prophets, swinging his ax with great enthusiasm and strength, suddenly felt the handle go light in his hands, and he saw to his dismay that the axhead had slipped off the haft and fallen into the waters of the Jordan. He looked down with consternation into the Jordan, whose waters are generally dark and troubled, and then, seeing Elisha standing near him, appealed to him and cried out, "Alas, master! for it was borrowed."

His distress was due partly to the fact that without his ax he could take no further part in building the new dormitory for the school of the prophets, and partly to the fact that his ax, no doubt like that of every other student at work in the forest that morning, was borrowed. Axes, we know, and weapons of iron were scarce and highly valued at that time in Israel's history. He had borrowed his ax, and now it was at the bottom of the Jordan. He was in distress because he had no money with which to purchase another, and he would be unable to return what he had borrowed. "Alas, master! for it was borrowed."

Elisha then came to his help. He asked him to point out

in the river the spot where the ax had disappeared beneath the waters. Then, asking for a stick, Elisha thrust it into the water, and, lo, the iron did something which iron had never done before and, I suppose, has never done since! "The iron did swim." Elisha then said to the young man, "Take it up to thee." The young man put out his hand and seized the axhead and, joyfully fastening it again to the haft, once more joined his companions in cutting down the trees for the new building. It was not the stick that brought the axhead to the surface of the river. The stick was only the sign and symbol of the divine power which Elisha was permitted to exercise.

"The iron did swim." This miracle was wrought to meet the need and relieve the distress of a young student in the school of the prophets on the banks of the Jordan River. It was as much of a miracle as those more striking and sensational miracles which are recorded in the Old Testament. God sent great wind and opened a pathway in the Red Sea by which the children of Israel passed over in safety on the march out of Egypt; and then he sent another great wind which brought the waters back again to overwhelm Pharaoh and his chariots. When the feet of the priests bearing the ark of the covenant came down into the waters of the Jordan, the waters of the river above, to the North, stood up in a heap, while the waters below flowed away into the Dead Sea, and the children of Israel, led by Joshua, passed over dry shod. These were mighty miracles wrought for the benefit of a whole nation. But the raising of the axhead by Elisha on this occasion was just as much a miracle, for, so far as natural laws were concerned, that axhead would be lying in the bed of the

Jordan to this day. It was a miracle wrought, not for a nation, or for a city, but to relieve the distress of one young man.

Sometimes I am asked if it is right for us when we pray to ask for other than spiritual and moral blessings and strength. Here we have the answer. God is interested in the ordinary affairs of our lives. From the time we get up in the morning until we go to bed at night, little matters, you might call them, engage our thought and time. Do not hesitate to ask God to guide you and to bless you and help you in the ordinary affairs of your life.

We might tarry on that part of the story—that is, the miracle, that the iron did swim—and take it as the starting place for a meditation on how our faith in God and in Christ enables us to deal with the adversities and trials and sorrows of life, and even with sin, when it has been forgiven, and thus, as it were, make iron to swim. But our chief concern will be with that cry of the young theological student, "Alas, master! for it was borrowed." I take this as a suggestion for the truth and fact that life in all its possessions, its opportunities, its talents, and its stay in this world is not our own, but is borrowed from the fountain of life and the Giver of all good. These sons of the prophets in the Jordan forest were engaged in building a greater house for the service of God. They were poor men and had to borrow axes for this enterprise. In this life we are all engaged in building a structure not for time, but for eternity. We are collecting material for the everlasting habitations, and all the instruments and implements with which we work are borrowed. They are not our own. They are loaned to us only for a season.

25

Isn't it strange
That princes and kings,
And clowns that caper
In sawdust rings,
And common people like you and me,
Are builders for Eternity.[1]

TIME IS BORROWED

I remember hearing my father, after he had passed a certain milestone in life, telling us now and then that he was "living on borrowed time"; that is, that he had passed the psalmist's allotted span. But that is true of all of us. We are all living on borrowed time. The infant that came into the world today, the little child in the home, the youth at school or college, the man in the midst of his years—all these, as well as the septuagenarian, the octogenarian, or the nonagenarian, are living on "borrowed time." Whether life at the present moment strikes one as bright or dark, joyous or sad, delightful or wretched, time is ever marching with relentless and steady pace to its appointed end for each one of us.

The clock of life is wound but once,
And no man has the power
To tell just when the hands will stop,
At late or early hour.[2]

In the nave of one of the great cathedrals of Europe there is a justly renowned astronomical clock. This clock, like the cathedral which houses it, has had many builders. It not only preaches from hour to hour on the solemn pas-

[1] Author unknown.
[2] Dr. George H. Candler.

sage of time, but is a monument to the greatness of the human mind. If the parts of this clock are kept in repair, the clock is so fabricated that it will mark the eclipses of the sun as long as the earth rolls. At noon the twelve apostles emerge and pass in reverent procession before the figure of Christ, who lifts his hand to bless them, while a cock flaps his wings and crows three times. In the center are four figures, each one holding a hammer, representing the four ages of life; and in the midst of them stands Death. At the first quarter a child lifts his little hammer and strikes the time. At the half hour rosy youth lifts his happy arm and strikes the second quarter. At the three-quarter hour sober manhood lifts his robust arm and strikes the third quarter. Then old age lifts his feeble and decrepit arm and with his hammer strikes the fourth quarter. When he has finished, Death lifts his hammer and strikes the hour. Childhood, youth, manhood, old age, death!

To stand and watch the figures strike the quarter hour, one after the other, and then to see Death lift his hammer and strike is subduing, impressive, solemnizing. You wonder when the final stroke will come for you. What are you doing with that portion of time which has been loaned to you? "So teach us to number our days, that we may apply our hearts unto wisdom."

OUR POSSESSIONS AND TALENTS ARE BORROWED

We hear men talk about "my house," "my business," "my land," "my possessions." Yet how true it is that all these things are not our own; they are loaned to us for a season. One whole book of the Bible, the book of Job, is of a nature to teach us that. When the sun rose one morning upon Job, he was the richest and greatest of all the men of the East. His flocks and herds covered the plains and whitened the hillsides. But when the sun set that night, Job was a pauper. He shaved his head and rent his mantle and fell down on the ground and worshiped, saying, "Naked came I out of my mother's womb, and naked shall I return thither: the Lord gave, and the Lord hath taken away; blessed be the name of the Lord." Not all have faith to meet adversity as Job met it, and to bless the Lord in all things; but none can deny the truth of what Job said, a truth that applies to all of us, "Naked came I out of my mother's womb, and naked shall I return thither."

Nebuchadnezzar, the king of Babylon, built a great city on the banks of the Euphrates twenty-four centuries ago. He built the city in the same general neighborhood where ages before men had assembled to build a tower and city so high that the top of it would reach to heaven. Where they had failed, Nebuchadnezzar thought he had succeeded.

According to the Greek historian Herodotus, the city was built in the form of a square fourteen miles long on every side. It had two protecting walls, one of them 373 feet high and 90 feet wide. The city had twenty-five gates of burnished brass, and great highways ran through the city, entering and leaving at these twenty-five gates. On an artificial hill, or mountain, four hundred feet high were the famous Hanging Gardens, or terraces, which Nebuchadnezzar had built so that in the otherwise flat plains of Babylon his wife might not be homesick for her native hills and mountains of Media. The city was splendid with palaces and temples, beautiful with gardens, abounding in tunnels and bridges and canals, and adorned with the spoils of conquered kingdoms. Let no one imagine that ours is the only age of great buildings or great structures. Babylon was the greatest capital the world had ever seen up to that time, and in certain respects it has never seen its equal.

You can see that proud monarch walking at evening along the wall of Babylon and looking down upon all its splendors as they were illuminated by the light of the setting sun, and saying to himself and to those with him, as Daniel relates, "Is not this great Babylon, that I have built for the house of the kingdom by the might of my power, and for the honour of my majesty?" But even while the word was in the king's mouth, a voice fell from heaven saying, "O king Nebuchadnezzar, . . . the kingdom is departed from thee." That very day Nebuchadnezzar was pulled from his throne and driven into the wilderness, where his body was wet with the dew of heaven; and he did eat grass as the ox until he learned that the Most High rules in the kingdom of men and gives to whomsoever he will. Nebuchadnezzar was a great king and ruler, but, so far as permanent possession was concerned, what happened to him is true of us all.

Jesus told us of another man, known as "the rich fool," who talked as Nebuchadnezzar did. His ground brought forth so plentifully that his only problem and trouble was how to bestow his goods and make use of his income. So this is what he said. Mark his use of the possessive first-person pronoun. "This will I do: I will pull down *my* barns, and build greater; and there will I bestow all *my* fruits and *my* goods. And I will say to *my* soul, Soul, thou hast much goods laid up for many years; take thine ease, eat, drink, and be merry." But, as quickly as God spoke to Nebuchadnezzar when he boasted of his possessions,

God said unto this man, "Thou fool, this night thy soul shall be required of thee: then whose shall those things be, which thou hast provided?"

If we could get all men—no, not all men, but all Christian men and women—to realize that all their earthly possessions are loaned to them of God, and that one day the loan will be required and recalled, no minister would have to stand up and plead for the support of a church. No hospital, asylum, home for little children, home for the aged, college for the training of youth, or any other good cause would lack the money for its support. The great Moslem conqueror Saladin, who fought with Richard the Lion-hearted about the walls of Acre, and whose tomb you can see at Damascus, left directions that he should be buried with his two hands extending out of his coffin, so that those empty hands might teach men that they brought nothing into the world and certainly can take nothing with them out of it.

OUR TALENTS ARE BORROWED

All the talents that you possess are borrowed for a season from heaven, the universal supply house. These talents and gifts are, as it were, axes loaned to us with which we may cut our way through to high character and to the kingdom of God. That is what Jesus taught us in the parables of the talents and the pounds. In the parable of the talents the man who was traveling into the far country gave to one servant five talents, to another two, and to another one, to everyone according to his ability. After a long time the lord of those servants returned from his journey and required a reckoning with his servants. The one who had received five talents brought another five; and the one who had received two talents gained two other talents. Both of them were rewarded by their master for their zeal and fidelity, and were promoted to higher places. But the man who had received the one talent had hidden his talent in the earth; and, bringing it, said to his lord, "Lo, there thou hast that is thine." He was stripped of the talent that he had and was punished as an unprofitable servant. In this parable Jesus teaches the difference in men's gifts and capacities, but he also shows their common responsibility.

In the parable of the pounds, however, which at first seems much the same, Jesus teaches not only our individual responsibility and accountability, but also the fact that all men have something with which they can serve God and their fellow man. The nobleman called his ten servants and delivered to each one of them the same amount, one pound. One, according to his ability, had gained ten pounds; another five pounds. But one, saying that he feared his Lord, brought back just the one pound which he had kept laid up in a napkin, and was judged accordingly.

It is a great thing when a young person awakens with a thrill to the realization that he has something within him with which he can serve God and his day and generation, and realizes also that all these gifts, like the talents and the pounds in the two parables, are borrowed from God. To men at Corinth who were inclined to boast about their gifts and talents Paul said, "What hast thou that thou didst not receive?" It is a sad thing to see men wasting their gifts and talents in pursuits that are unworthy of the soul.

There is a sadness, indeed, in the wasting of talents in dissipation and wrong living. But there is also a sadness in the devoting of our talents and gifts to things which are not of themselves sinful and shameful, but which are of secondary importance compared with the Kingdom of God. Everyone has it in him today to do something for that kingdom of God which the King of that Kingdom said it was our business to seek first of all.

OUR OPPORTUNITIES ARE BORROWED

Our families, our loved ones, our friends, are opportunities. Fathers and mothers, children, brothers and sisters, husbands and wives, are opportunities for the investment of affection and fidelity and loving service. Yet the tendency on the part of many is to take our best friends and companions for granted, as a part, as it were, of the fixed furniture of life, not realizing that they are loaned to us for a season. Then suddenly, while we are "busy, here and there," they are gone. They have vanished on life's horizon, and not even an Elisha has the power to call them back to us. Sooner than we think, these loans are called in.

> How little time, alas, have we
> To gentle be and kind,
> Ere we shall mingle with the vagrant winds,
> The never-sleeping sea.
> Then, ever searching, shall we ever find,
> I you, you me.[3]

Many years ago in an old cemetery in America's oldest city, St. Augustine, I came upon the grave of a young soldier. On the stone was an inscription put there by his

[3] Author unknown.

mourning parents, which said, in substance: "We return to God our son who was loaned to us for a season."

Life's greatest opportunity is the opportunity for salvation of the soul, the opportunity of repentance toward God and faith in the Lord Jesus Christ. This immortal soul is not your own. You have borrowed it from heaven. It was loaned you for a season, and one day the loan will be called in. As Jesus said, "This night thy soul shall be required of thee." Near the end of the great twelfth chapter of Ecclesiastes we come upon this statement: "Then shall the dust return to the earth as it was: and the spirit . . . unto God who gave it."

When God calls in this divine loan, our soul, and requires it of us, what will your soul be like when you return it to him? Your soul was given you not that you might pollute it with lust and sensuality and drink, or defile and corrupt it with avarice and selfishness, or encrust it with hatred, but that you might do the will of God. And yet it is obvious that a universal calamity has overtaken the soul of man. The best that any of us can say is, "Alas, my master, it was borrowed! Now it is lost!" So Jesus said, "What shall it profit a man, if he shall gain the whole world, and lose his own soul?" And that other searching question also, "What shall a man give in exchange for his soul?" That is, if he has sinned against the soul and scarred it and stained it, and so lost it, what can he give or do that will get him back his soul? There is nothing that he can give or do. But that question that Christ asked, and which no man can answer, "What shall a man give in exchange for his soul?" Christ himself has answered. He answered it in the sublime tragedy of the cross, whereon

33

he gave himself for our souls' redemption, and where he came to seek and to save that which was lost.

That son of the prophets could do nothing to get his ax back. But God, through the prophet Elisha, intervened; and when the stick was thrust by the prophet into the water, the iron did swim. When the blood-stained wood of the cross is thrust down into our hearts, it finds and recovers for us the soul. So even the iron of sin is made to swim! Have you called upon God, as the son of the prophets called upon Elisha? Have you committed your soul unto God? Can you say, "I know whom I have believed, and am persuaded that he is able to keep that which I have committed unto him against that day"?

III

"Stings in their tails . . ."

Rev. 9:10

THE DISGUISE OF SIN

PEOPLE LIKE TO SEE A SPECTACLE. THEY RUSH TO THE latest pageant, parade, and movie. But here in the Apocalypse we have the greatest spectacle of all, the drama of the ages, the struggle between good and evil, between the Church and the world. The actors on one side are God, Christ, holy angels, and redeemed men. On the other side, the Devil and his angels.

As page after page opens, we catch the noise and tumult of the conflict and see the struggles of the contending armies. The one through whom we are permitted to see this is John, the prisoner of Patmos. The great vision opens with Christ standing amid the seven golden candlesticks. To John he gives a message to each of the seven churches. Then a door is opened in heaven, and John beholds a great throne, girt with a rainbow and guarded by seven lamps, which are the seven Spirits of God, and the four beasts, having respectively the face of the lion, the calf, the man, and the eagle. A seven-sealed book is brought forth. But none is found worthy to break and loose the seals thereof. This book contains the destiny of man and the Church. But when all others have failed, the "Lamb slain from the foundation of the world" comes forth and takes the book out of the hand of him that sits upon the throne, and to the magnificent accompaniment of the praise of the whole creation he opens one by one the seven seals.

The first seal is opened, and the white horse and his rider, the Victorious One, go forth conquering and to conquer; the second, and the red horse, War, goes forth. The third, and the black horse, Famine, goes forth. The fourth, and the pale horse with Death astride goes forth. When the fifth seal is opened, the souls of the martyrs, clad in white robes, appear before God. The sixth seal is opened with a great earthquake and with the stars falling from heaven. The great multitude of the redeemed, with the Lamb standing in the midst of them, appears in heaven. Hunger and thirst shall be no more, "for the Lamb which is in the midst of the throne shall feed them, and shall lead them unto living fountains of waters: and God shall wipe away all tears from their eyes."

When the seventh seal is opened, there is silence in heaven for half an hour. Its unspeakable harmonies, the voices of Judgment and of Doom, the ascriptions of the redeemed, the lamentations of the lost—all were silenced. At the end of this pause in the history of the universe the seven angels with the seven trumpets stand before God. The first angel sounds, and there are hail and fire, mingled with blood, and the trees and the grass are burned up. The second sounds, and a burning mountain is cast into the sea, and the third part of the sea becomes blood. The third sounds, and the star Wormwood falls from heaven upon the waters and the rivers, and they become wormwood. The fourth sounds, and the third part of the heavens is darkened. The fifth sounds, and there falls from heaven a star to which is given the key to the bottomless pit.

With this key the fallen star opens the abyss, and there pours forth smoke as of a great furnace, obscuring the light of the sun. Out of the smoking cloud comes a vast army of locusts, or scorpions, with crowns of gold on their heads, but with stings in their tails. The leader of this host is the angel of the abyss, Apollyon, and to this army of scorpions is given the power to sting and torment men and inflict such intense sufferings that they shall long for death but not find it.

THE DECEITFULNESS OF SIN

We take this great vision of the Apocalypse as setting forth the disguise and deceitfulness of sin, the pleasures of sin for a season, and sin's power to hurt and ruin the souls of men. The scorpions had crowns of gold on their head, but their sting was in their tail. The disguise of evil is shown, first of all, in anti-Christian theories and systems of government for the organization of human society. These hold out great promise for "the better life." Man's material possessions are to be vastly increased. Every man is to be his own master and sit unmolested under his own vine and fig tree. But too often these Utopian schemes ignore the differences in talents men possess, and discount thrift and energy and honesty. This "better life" ignores the spiritual side of man, and either ignores God or rebels against him and denies him. Whitaker Chambers said of Communism—and he ought to know; for many years he was its dupe and tool—that the core and heart of it is the denial of God, the displacement of God as the central fact of the universe, and the substitution of man as the central fact, with man's life and destiny confined to this present world and to material things only.

Millions in our day have been led astray by these social theories. They have seen only the glitter of the golden crown and have not seen the poisonous and deadly sting. Millions of Communists in China and in North Korea embraced the doctrine of Communism with vast enthusiasm. What has it brought to them? Starvation, hunger, and death by the hundreds of thousands upon the bloodsoaked mountains of Korea. The crowns of gold which they saw in the distance and which infatuated them have dissolved in misery, and now they are feeling the sting of death. Social theories and plans which leave out God are like the scorpions which came out of hell— crowns of gold on their heads, but a deadly sting in their tails.

Thomas Carlyle, once hearing men discuss, as if it were only an academic matter, certain radical social theories, reminded them that there were those in France in the eighteenth century who liked to discuss the theories of Rousseau as if they were just theories. But the day came when new editions of Rousseau's works appeared bound in the skins of the very men who had lightly dismissed them. Robespierre was one of the architects of the Reign of Terror in France. In time he himself fell a victim to the terror which he had let loose upon France. On the day of Robespierre's execution a French peasant, gazing upon his severed head, exclaimed, "Yes, Robespierre, there is a God!"

Crowns of gold and tails with death in their sting have appeared not infrequently in the history of the church. The Apostle Paul in one of his letters to the Thessalonians speaks of those who have become the victims of "a strong delusion, that they should believe a lie." That has happened often in the history of Christianity. Unbelief appears to the church with a crown of gold on its head. It introduces itself under the guise of progress and liberty, or speaks great, swelling words about emancipation, church unity, and brotherhood. This new form of Christianity was to win the adherence of the scholars and the scientists and secure the enthusiasm of the students in colleges and universities. But instead of that, what we speak of today as "modernism" has brought a terrible blight upon the church. The apples of gold which it held out before men have turned out to be apples of Sodom.

THE PLEASURES OF SIN

There are, indeed, pleasures of sin; but they are only "for a season." Such as these pleasures are, the sin must be repeated for one to experience them; and the oftener it is repeated, the less is the pleasure. This is a path which is blazed through the Bible for all those who would be made wise. The tempter invited the woman to look upon the forbidden fruit, and asked her if it was not good to look upon, and assured her that if she ate of it, the taste would be just as good, and even better, than the look. If they ate of it, he told her, her eyes and the eyes of Adam would be opened. And so it proved to be. But not in the way they had expected, for their eyes were opened "to good lost and evil got."

Balaam, the eloquent seer of Mesopotamia, wanted desperately the gold that the king of Moab offered him if he would come and curse Israel. He refused the first time; and when he went the second time—no doubt hoping that this time he could curse the people and get Balak's gold—instead of cursing them, he pronounced under divine inspiration a great blessing upon them and forecast their destiny in terms of grandeur unsurpassed in the Bible. Listening to the music of those predictions, we might conclude that Balaam was now beyond all temptation to seek after the gold of Balak. Alas, that was not true. Unable to curse the people, Balaam proceeded by a wicked plot to make the people curse themselves by immorality and sin with a heathen people; and, in the end, instead of dying the "death of the righteous," as he had fervently prayed he might do, he fell in battle fighting with the enemies of Israel. Balak's gold wore a crown of gold; but the sting of death was in it.

Joshua had declared the fallen Jericho "out of bounds," for the people of Israel, and its spoils were forbidden. But when Achan stole out from his tent at night and, searching amid the ruins of Jericho, saw the flash of the silver and gold and the goodly Babylonish garments, he coveted these spoils and hid them under his tent. "No one," he said to himself, "will know. Not even Joshua himself." But God knew; and soon Joshua knew and Israel knew, and Achan and his family fell beneath the stones of judgment. The gold and the garments had a sting in their tail.

When Gehazi, the servant of Elisha, heard Elisha refuse the costly gifts that Naaman, who had been healed of his leprosy, offered to him in gratitude for his healing, he said to himself, "If Elisha doesn't want that silver and gold and those garments, I can make good use of them." With a clever lie he persuaded Naaman to bestow the gifts upon him and hid them in his house. But when he appeared before Elisha, Elisha said to him, "The leprosy

therefore of Naaman shall cleave unto thee . . . forever."
And he went out from his presence a leper white as snow!
It seemed good to crafty Jacob to deceive his half-blind
father, Isaac, and cheat his brother Esau out of the blessing by putting the skin of the kid of the goats on his hands
and on his neck and pretending that he was Esau. But,
alas, the day came when his own sons appeared before
him, when he too was an old man, and held up before
him the rent and torn robe of many colors which Joseph
had worn and which they had dipped in blood of *another*
kid of the goats and told their father that a wild beast
had slain Joseph. The wicked deceit that Jacob had practiced upon his father now came back upon his own head.

Judas Iscariot came to the place where he thought that
the thirty pieces of silver which the scribes and Pharisees
offered him were worth more to him than the fellowship
of Jesus. But after the betrayal when he heard that Jesus
had been sentenced to death by the court of the high priest,
and that Pilate had delivered him up to be crucified, those
thirty pieces of silver burned his hand and burned his
soul; and he went out and hanged himself. That is the
natural history and sequence of sin—crowns of gold on
its head, but the sting of death in its tail. The natural
history of transgression was set forth truly and plainly by
James when he said: "Every man is tempted, when he
is drawn away of his own lust, and enticed. Then when
lust hath conceived, it bringeth forth sin: and sin, when
it is finished, bringeth forth death." That is always the
natural history of evil. The wise man said, "Stolen waters
are sweet, . . . but he knoweth not that the dead are there;
and that are guests are in the depths of hell."

The pleasures of strong drink for a moment, at least,

must be real. It loosens the tongue. It makes the dumb speak. It makes the eye sparkle. But that is only for a season. That is only the beginning. This is the end: "Wine is a mocker, strong drink is raging: and whosoever is deceived thereby is not wise." "Look now not on the wine when it is red, when it giveth its color in its cup; when it moveth itself aright. At the last it biteth like a serpent, and stingeth like an adder."

Robert Burns, who made considerable experiment with certain kinds of sin, gave this as his verdict:

> But pleasures are like poppies spread,
> You seize the flow'r, its bloom is shed;
> Or like the snowfall in the river,
> A moment white—then melts for ever.[1]

Lord Byron, too, experimented widely and deeply with the pleasures of sin, and here are the lines he wrote on his thirty-sixth birthday:

> My days are in the yellow leaf;
> The flowers and fruits of love are gone;
> The worm, the canker, and the grief
> Are mine alone![2]

Let us pass now over this battlefield where the despoiled and the dead lie, and let us see, perchance, if we can identify some of them. This man in middle life, by wisdom and prudence, by following the path of the just, brought himself to influence and affluence. But now, alas, here he

[1] "Tam O'Shanter."
[2] "On This Day I Complete My Thirty-Sixth Year."

lies, stripped and dishonored. Why? Because, after years of abstinence and care, he fancied that it would be safe for him to experiment, just a little, with the pleasures of sin. It was to be only for a season; but this is the end. And here is this young man, of whose future accomplishments the brightest hopes were entertained. He was to stand high, and take a leading place in the church, the law, or in the world of affairs. But now, alas, his voice can never ring out on the side of righteousness, and he will be remembered not by what he was, but by what he might have been. The scorpion stung him with its tail.

There is the story of a clever fabricator who designed a goblet so that when the drinker reached the bottom, a coiled serpent suddenly struck out with its dripping fangs. This is a strong figure and illustration; but, alas, not half as strong as life, the great teacher, declares from day to day.

It is said of Moses that at the critical period of his life he chose "to suffer affliction with the people of God" rather "than to enjoy the pleasures of sin for a season." The significant thing there is that Moses *chose*. Everyone must choose. Life is a moral choice and decision. The sure way to make the right choice and the happy decision is to choose Christ. In the light of his presence the false crowns on the heads of temptation and evil topple and fade and disappear, and the teeth and sting of sin are made visible. To choose Christ, for day and night, for plenty and for want, for better or for worse, is to choose now, and at the end, happiness and eternal life.

IV

"Dig now in the wall."
Ezek. 8:8

WHAT ARE YOU IN THE DARK?

THE PROPHET EZEKIEL, A CAPTIVE AMONG THE JEWS ON
the banks of the Chebar in far-off Babylon, saw a hand
stretched forth out of the flame of fire. This hand lifted
him up and transported him to the court of the Temple
at Jerusalem. There he saw, set up in the sacred precincts,
an image of jealousy; that is, a heathen idol which pro-
voked the righteous indignation and jealousy of Jehovah.
This was bad, but what was to come was worse. Ezekiel
saw a hole in the wall of the inner court of the Temple.
Obeying his angelic guide, he dug in this hole and enlarged
it, so that he was able to pass through it. Then he came
to a second wall, in which was a door, and through the
door he passed into a large chamber. The walls of this
chamber of imagery were decorated with the unclean
symbols and likenesses of heathen worship. Before these
filthy pictures stood seventy elders of Israel, swinging
their censers and mumbling their adoration and incanta-
tions. The angel said to Ezekiel, "Hast thou seen what
the ancients of the house of Israel do in the dark, every
man in the chambers of his imagery? for they say, The
Lord seeth us not; the Lord hath forsaken the earth."

Shocked at this disclosure of secret apostasy and idolatry, Ezekiel was to see even greater abominations. He

followed the angel out of the secret chamber, and near the gate of the Temple beheld Jewish women weeping openly for Tammuz. Tammuz was the Oriental equivalent of Adonis, the paramour of Venus; and the rites of this worship were carried out with unbridled licentiousness. At Baalbek today one can see the beautiful ruins of the Temple of Venus; and, learning what was done there, one sadly contrasts the beauty of architecture with the hideousness of the worship. One realizes, too, the immense progress that has been made in religious worship since the time when religion was openly associated with sensuality and licentiousness.

As a climax to this series of revelations of the apostasy of God's people, Ezekiel was shown twenty-five men standing near the door of the Temple, with their backs to the Temple and their faces toward the east, worshiping the sun!

Then came the pronouncement of judgment and the portrayal of retribution. Six men appeared, each armed with a slaughter weapon. Then a seventh appeared, clothed in white linen, with a writer's inkhorn by his side. He made a round of the city and put a mark on the forehead of every man who still was loyal to Jehovah and sighed and cried for the abominations done in the city. The world will not "go to the dogs" completely until the man with the inkhorn is unable to find in our cities a single person who "sighs and cries" for the abominations which are done. When the man with the inkhorn had concluded his census of the faithful and the righteous, then the six men armed with the slaughter weapons went forth and smote all who had not the mark on their brow.

This was a vision which Ezekiel saw. But it was a

vision in action; and therefore it is a parable of life. The application is first of all to the national and religious condition of Israel. But as national character and the religious life of the nation can express themselves only through individuals, we shall all find something that is timeless and abiding for our warning and our profit in this parable. It shows us, in the first place, the progressive nature of sin, and how one sin leads to others and to worse. In the second place, it is a picture of the wickedness and the doom of hypocrisy; and in the third place, it sets forth the power and the reality of the hidden life of thought, fancy, and imagination.

THE PROGRESSIVE NATURE OF SIN

The prophet was shown a hole in the wall. It was not large, but when it was made larger, it opened to a subterranean chamber of infamy and shame. There are certain conditions and situations which lead as naturally and as inevitably to sin and guilt as the sunset leads to the night and to the darkness. One small spot or focus of infection in a given body, if disregarded, will spread corruption through the whole body. What of the "hole in the wall" of your life? Is there a weakness or evasion of truth, some secretly indulged habit which is steadily leading the soul down to a chamber of transgression and corruption? Is there neglect of duty or of religious habits, which opens the way for something worse? A man who had fallen into deep sin and had amazed his friends and those who trusted in him by what he had done, said, "I fell when I stopped praying."

On the campus of the theological seminary at Princeton are many ancient, stately, and beautiful elm trees. Every spring I used to watch the tree surgeons at their work of pruning and trimming and cutting away the dead limbs and branches and pouring their black cement into the holes and spaces where decay and corruption had commenced. It is not otherwise with the tree of one's life and character. Where there is a hole, repair it, or it will lead to something worse.

THE MISERY OF HYPOCRISY

There were two kinds of worship being carried on at Jerusalem: first of all, the official public worship in the Temple courts; but down below a private, secret, and idolatrous worship. The worship above was just a sham worship. The real worship was what was done in the chambers of imagery, where the seventy elders were swinging their censers before the unclean pictures of the heathen gods and goddesses.

In the life of every person who aims at that which is good and endeavors to follow Christ there is bound to be a degree of failure and inconsistency. His reach will always be higher than his grasp. We must all fall short of our highest aims, and there will always be a hiatus between our professions and our best achievements.

But it is not this shortcoming that is meant when we speak of hypocrisy. Rather, it is the deliberate living of a lie; the worshiping above ground, or pretending to worship, that which is good and holy, while underground, in the secret but real life, we worship that which is altogether different.

Once on an August Sabbath I attended a gray Norman church on the cliffs at Tintagel on the coast of Cornwall, the reputed seat of King Arthur and his knights. The wind carried the spray from the waves breaking against the iron cliffs clear up to the windows of the little church, where a handful of the people had assembled for worship. The sermon by the rector was memorable for its six-minute brevity, but also for one expression which I have never forgotten. He said that we really worship only that which we ourselves desire to be. The real worship of life is in the desire of the heart.

There is no doubt about the wickedness and guilt of deliberate hypocrisy and insincerity. More than anything else, it seems to prove the fall of man and the influence of Satan over his nature. Nor is there any doubt about the punishment which waits upon hypocrisy. The men with the slaughter weapons slew the elders of Israel who stood before the people as the representatives of the divine law and yet at the same time secretly practiced the foul rites of Egypt and Babylon. The unmasking of hypocrisy has been a favorite theme of the dramatist and the novelist. It is but an expression of the conviction that ultimately hypocrisy shall be unmasked and every hidden thing brought to light.

Nor is there any doubt as to the misery of the hypocrite, the man of double life. Always he is under the necessity of trying to make two hostile and opposite lives harmonize and coincide. A friend brought up on a western Pennsylvania farm has told me that the best of dogs will sometimes be taken with the fever of sheep killing. This killing is always done at night. The guilty dog will always endeavor to tempt other dogs to go with him, and, if possible, he will lay the blame at their door. When this madness of sheep killing is on him, the dog will assume during the day, at the house and around the barn, an unusually

48

genial and friendly air. Thus, even animal natures seem to share in the hypocrisy which has invaded human nature.

THE POWER OF THOUGHT AND IMAGINATION

A man's character is what he is in the dark. We are the inhabitants of two worlds—the outer and visible world of form and speech and look and action, and the inner and invisible world of thought, desire, and imagination. Where do you live? In a house of brick or stone or timber, on this street or on that avenue? No. You live in a house men never see. The real temple is your own heart, and on its walls by the brush of fancy and imagination are painted the pictures before which you really bow down and worship. This temple of our hidden thought-life has, as Hawthorne put it, "upper stories and apartments where the inhabitants of earth may hold converse with those of the moon; and beneath our feet are gloomy cells which communicate with the infernal regions, and where monsters and chimeras are kept in confinement and fed with all unwholesomeness." Every one of us has an observatory which looks outward and upward toward heaven and the stars; and every one, too, has a ladder which leads down to hell.

The hidden world of imagination and thought is the real life and the real world because, in the first place, it is the sincere and actual life. There good is done for the sake of good, evil for the sake of evil. There no considerations of fear or shame hold us back, no thought of what another will say or think, or what effect this will have upon our prospects and our prosperity. In this hidden realm there is no shamming or pretending. There we are exactly what we are. On a church board whereon was displayed one of those brief sayings calculated to arrest and impress the casual reader as he passes by, I read this, "You are not what you think you are; but you *are* what you *think*." As a man "thinketh in his heart, so is he." In this hidden realm all disguise and pretense are thrown off, and we worship what we really desire and admire. There is a legend of an ancient despot, Gyges, who would sometimes bestow upon a favorite a ring which had the effect of making him invisible. He himself was in real flesh and blood existence, but the ring made him invisible to others. Sometimes we wonder just what people would be like, what they would say, what they would do, if they possessed the magic, disguising ring of Gyges!

Now we understand why it is that the Bible always lays such emphasis upon the heart and its life, and how it was that Christ placed the emphasis upon what a man thinks and desires in his heart. The old law, Christ said, condemned and punished the act. But Christ and his law condemn and punish the thought and the desire. The old law condemned the murderer. Christ condemns the heart which hates, for without hate there is no murder. The old law condemned the adulterer. Christ condemns the person of impure desires.

The life of thought and desire is the real life because, in the second place, it is the creative life. It is the creative life on the good side. All things noble and worthy are done first in this workshop and factory of thought. And so it is with all things that are unseemly and evil. There is nothing in an outside, external object which, in itself, has any power to hurt you or defile you, except by the co-operation of your own inner life of imagination and desire. A spark falling upon ice or stone merely goes out; but

50

if it fall upon powder, there is immediate combustion and explosion. Christ expressed this when he said that the things that proceed out of a man, and not the things which go into him, are those that defile him. When he was asked to interpret this, Jesus replied: "That which cometh out of the man, that defileth the man. For from within, out of the heart of men, proceed evil thoughts, adulteries, fornications, murders, thefts, covetousness, wickedness, deceit, lasciviousness, an evil eye, blasphemy, pride, foolishness: All these evil things come from within, and defile the man."

The creative power of the thought world is strikingly demonstrated by the fact that for the transgressions which are done by word and deed, and which sometimes shock and amaze men, there has always been a preparatory pollution in the realm of thought. There probably is never such a thing as a "sudden" fall. It has always been antedated and prepared for by a fall in the hidden life.

Of all the truths of the moral and spiritual world I suppose that this with which I am dealing, the power of the thought life upon the outward life and the irreparable injury which can be done by wrong thinking, is the most neglected. I read recently a statement by an essayist who said that only twice in his life had he heard this truth mentioned in religious instruction. Undoubtedly one half, if not three fourths, of the art of Christian living consists in the shunning of temptation; and the first place to shun temptation is where it is always the most dangerous and works the greatest injury, and that is in the life of the heart.

The aids to right thinking, to the bringing of every thought, as Paul puts it, into captivity to Christ, are

51

industry, good associations, good books, and a determination to keep inviolate the temple of one's inner life. What shall we think of the man who will do in the secret chambers of his own imagination without shame or self-reproach what he would be ashamed to do in the sight of others? That means that he is so despicable as to have more respect for the thought and opinion of strangers than he has for himself. The work of the Holy Spirit is too commonly neglected by Christians, and in this realm especially, for the Holy Spirit is the inspirer of every good and noble thought. Ask, then, for his indwelling.

But what shall we say to those who may wish that they had heard and heeded such advice long ago? What shall we say for those who have defiled with evil thinking the walls of the chambers of imagination? What can be done with this stained past? By the grace of repentance the walls of the soul can be redecorated, and whatsoever things are lovely, pure, and of good report can take the place of the things that are ugly and unseemly.

In some parts of Europe you can see where pictures and symbols of the Gospels and of the Christian life have been painted over heathen frescoes of unspeakable shame and indecency. So the brush of repentance can decorate anew the chambers of the soul. "Create in me a clean heart, O God; and renew a right spirit within me."

V

"For the bed is shorter than that
a man can stretch himself on it."

Isa. 28:20

THIS WORLD TOO SMALL
FOR MAN

ELEUSIS IS A TOWN IN GREECE ON THE ROAD FROM
Athens to Corinth. Near Eleusis was the stronghold of
a notorious robber and brigand, Procrustes. In his castle
Procrustes had two beds, one long and the other short.
When he brought his prisoners to his castle, he made them
sleep in one of those beds. If the prisoner was a long man,
he thrust him into the short bed and cut off his extremities
to make him fit the bed. If he was a short man, he put
him in the long bed and stretched his body to the length
of the bed. Hence the saying, "the bed of Procrustes."

Here in our text we have a bed like the short bed of
Procrustes, a very uncomfortable bed, too short for the
man who tries to sleep in it, and its coverings too narrow
to cover the sleeper. Nothing could be more wretched
or uncomfortable than to try to sleep in a bed that is too
short for you to stretch yourself on it. Anyone who has
tried to do that will remember what a miserable night he
spent. Likewise nothing could be more uncomfortable
than to try to sleep on a cold night on a bed where the
blanket is not sufficient to cover the body. Perhaps, as I

have, you have had to sleep with one of your brothers, who took most of the blanket.

This is the striking metaphor that Isaiah, that eloquent master of metaphors, makes use of to describe a plan of life, national or personal, that leaves out God. Such a plan is a bed too short for the man to stretch himself on, and its covering is too scanty to give warmth to the body.

A NATION THAT LEAVES GOD OUT

The immediate application of this metaphor of Isaiah was to the national and international situations which then existed in Judah and Jerusalem. Instead of relying upon God and upon righteousness of conduct and the policies which Isaiah had outlined for them, the leaders of the people at Jerusalem had sought alliances with foreign nations, now with Assyria and now with Egypt. Isaiah scornfully told them that such alliances were only a refuge of lies which would be swept away in the hail of judgment. They were a covenant with death which would be broken and an agreement with hell which could not stand. All these measures of defense would turn out to be totally inadequate. They would prove to be like a bed too short for the man who lies on it, or a blanket too narrow for the man who tries to wrap himself in it.

Like everything else in the Bible, this is a timeless truth. Judah, Assyria, and Egypt, as they existed then, have all disappeared, but the message of Isaiah is still timely. Among the powerful dictators who recently bestrode the earth like Colossi, which one of them gave any recognition in his proud and boasting utterances to the moral law, to the kingdom of God, to the authority of

Jesus Christ? Nowhere did you hear such a note. Nor is it only in the foreign nations that this is true. To a certain extent it is sadly true of our own country. Which one of the political leaders do we hear striking the moral note and calling the nation back to God?

When Paul at the harbor of Fair Havens in Crete warned the centurion who had command of the soldiers and prisoners that it would be dangerous to attempt to proceed further on their voyage, and that if they did so there would be great hurt and damage, not only to the ship, but to their lives, the centurion "believed the master and the owner of the ship, more than those things which were spoken by Paul." He took the advice of the experts, or supposed experts, in navigation, and dismissed the advice of Paul, the man of God. The result was shipwreck. In our own national policies today the centurions who are in command of the national ship gave their whole attention to the experts in finance, economics, science, and politics. The opinion of the man of God and the message of God receive little consideration. The connection between national morality and national prosperity is almost totally ignored, and that in spite of the repeated lessons of history. It is strange that men should be so blind as to think that they can build enduringly on any foundation save that of righteousness. Present events, as well as the history of the past, demonstrate what the future again will demonstrate, that the history of the world is the judgment of the world. The nations that forget God shall be cast into hell. Sir Joseph Stamp, well-known British economist, speaking at a Canadian university on the solution of the world's industrial, commercial, and financial problems, said this: "I suspect any solution that does not stand an ethical test. The Sermon on the Mount is perhaps too fine a sieve for today, but the Decalogue is a mesh that can do thorough work. That, at least, we have not outgrown in standard. Do not think that education weans you from the spiritual law either."

Henry W. Grady, the famous editor of the *Atlanta Constitution* and a noted orator, speaking at a dinner in Boston on the strength of the nation, related how he had stood on the Capitol hill in Washington, and how his heart beat quick, "as I looked at the towering marble of my country's Capitol, and a mist gathered in my eyes as I thought of its tremendous significance; and I felt that the sun in all its course could not look down on a better sight than that majestic home of a Republic that has taught the world its best lessons of liberty."

A few days later he went to visit a friend in a farmhouse which he describes as "a simple, unpretentious house, set about with great trees and encircled by meadow and field, rich with the promise of harvest." That evening, after the work about the farm was done and the cows had come down the lane with the children singing after them, the family were assembled in the living room, where the father "took the Bible from the table and called them to their knees, while he closed the record of that day by calling down God's blessing on that simple home." "While I gazed" said Grady, "the vision of the marble Capitol faded; forgotten were its treasuries and its majesties; and I said, 'surely here in the homes of the people, lodge at last the strength and the responsibility of this government, the hope and the promise of this Republic.' " Our nation is no stronger than its faith. "Except the Lord build the house, they labour in vain that build it: except the Lord keep the city, the watchman waketh but in vain."

A LIFE THAT LEAVES OUT OTHERS

Although Isaiah's metaphor is solemn and striking when applied to national life, it has a still deeper meaning when applied to personal life. A plan of life which leaves out God and prayer and worship and faith is a plan of life, which in the end will prove totally inadequate for the needs of the soul. It will be like a bed too short for the man who tries to stretch himself on it, and like a covering that is too narrow and scanty to protect the man who seeks to wrap himself in it.

A plan of life which does not take in others, which does not consider his neighbor, is a plan too short and too narrow for man's soul. If we would live largely and nobly we cannot live to ourselves. The word of Holy Writ, "None of us to himself," is forever true. They who attempt to lead such a life must in the end atone for it in unhappiness and loneliness. The message of Christ and the hopes of the Christian life will not fit into such a plan. Paul struck the true note for life when he exclaimed that he was debtor to the whole world. The trouble with so many today is that they are thinking altogether of what the world owes them, what the country owes them, what the government owes them; and not what they owe to others and to the world. On beautiful Princes Street in Edinburgh is the monument to the great Scottish preacher Thomas Guthrie, who was a friend of the forgotten and outcast and of destitute children. These were his favorite verses:

I live to hail the season,
　　By gifted ones foretold,
When men shall rule by reason,
　　And not alone by gold;
When man to man united,
And every wrong thing righted,
The whole world shall be lighted,
　　As Eden was of old.

I live for those who love me,
　　For those who know me true;
For the heaven that smiles above me,
　　And waits my spirit too;
For the cause that lacks assistance,
For the wrong that needs resistance,
For the future in the distance,
　　And the good that I can do.[1]

A LIFE THAT LEAVES OUT THE CROSS

Self-righteousness is another plan that is too narrow
for man. This is a bed upon which a great host lie down
—the bed of morality, the bed of self-righteousness and
good works. Men measure themselves by themselves and
conclude that they can get along without the righteousness of God which is in Christ. The Sermon on the Mount,
they say, is their religion, forgetting that perfection is
the standard and requirement of that sermon. "I am as
good," says this man, "as the average run of men, and if
there have been some mistakes and transgressions in my
life, God in his mercy can overlook that." So they think
they can afford to ignore and neglect that great and only

[1] George L. Banks, "What I Live For."

provision for righteousness and justice as proclaimed in the Cross of Christ.

But this is a bed that is too short for man. His own righteousness is a covering that is too narrow for him to wrap himself in it. The total inadequacy of such a plan of life and such a plan of salvation is best demonstrated and illustrated, not by the marred and stained and broken lives of those who so often boast of their reliance upon good works, but by those who have achieved the highest place in the realm of moral righteousness. Men like Job, who cried out, "If I wash myself with snow water, . . . yet shalt thou plunge me in the ditch"; and Isaiah, who, when he saw the glory of God in the temple where the seraphim covered their faces and the foundations of the temple shook and the house was filled with smoke, fell on his face and exclaimed, "Woe is me! for I am undone; because I am a man of unclean lips, and I dwell in the midst of a people of unclean lips: for mine eyes have seen the King, the Lord of hosts"; and men like Paul, who in the midst of almost unparalleled and unprecedented struggles for the righteousness of the law, for salvation through moral character, cried out, "O wretched man that I am! who shall deliver me from the body of this death?" Or some of you may think of prophetic and apostolic lives lived in the range of your own vision, a godly father and mother whose plane of living, whose walk with God, appears now so far beyond your own emulation or attainment, yet who themselves from the serene heights of their walk with God would have been the last to claim any merit of their own but ever put their reliance upon the merit of Christ, who died for their sins, and whose righteousness became their righteousness by faith. Any other righteousness but that, any other plan for meeting the demand that God makes upon our soul, is too meager and short and narrow. It is in the end a bed of torture, not a bed of sleep; and our vaunted robe of self-righteousness turns out to be but a miserable rag.

A LIFE THAT LEAVES OUT HEAVEN

In a plan of life which takes in this world only, we have again a plan that is altogether too short and too meager for man; and yet, when we come down to it, how many plan their lives with regard to this world only, as if this were the only world, and as if this were the only life! They never taste, as the Apostle put it, of the "powers of the world to come." Their whole plan of life's campaign is based on the theory, "One world at a time; and if there is another life, we can let that go until we come to it."

A friend once said to me of certain persons, "They are trying to get more out of this world than there is in it." Such a plan is not great enough for man. For what is man? He is not a termite, an insect crawling over the leaves of the tree of pleasure in this world, nor a bit of dust blown over the face of the desert, nor an ox which eats the grass of the field and is satisfied and thinks not of God and of life to come. Man is something greater than that. He is a son of God, made a little lower than the angels, crowned with the honor of his creation and with the glory of his possible destiny. How sad and ignoble, then, is a plan of life that fits man in this world only; for, as Pascal said in that noble passage which a competent critic, Dr. Albert Guerard, has declared the finest in French prose: "Man is but a reed, the feeblest thing in nature; but he is a reed that thinks. It needs not that the universe arise to crush him. An exhalation, a drop of water suffices to destroy him. But were the universe to crush man, man is nobler than the universe, for he knows that he dies, and the universe, even in prevailing against him knows not its power."

In his autobiography W. H. Hudson, author of the widely read books, *Green Mansions* and *Days in Patagonia,* relates an incident of his early life in South America. The family dog, Caesar, had died, and was lowered into a grave which had been dug for him. The schoolmaster looked around on the boys assembled at the grave and said solemnly, "That's the end. Every dog has its day; and so has every man; and the end is the same for both. We die like old Caesar and are put into the ground, and have the earth shovelled over us." That is the bed upon which the materialist lies down. But it is too short a bed for a man in whose heart God hath "set eternity."

Bismarck, Germany's famous "Iron Chancellor," when speaking one day on the subject of immortality with our ambassador to Germany, Andrew D. White, said: "I do not doubt it even for a moment. This life is too sad, too incomplete, to satisfy our highest aspirations and desires. It is meant to be a struggle to ennoble us. Can the struggle be in vain? I think not. Final perfection I believe in. A perfection which God has in store for us." Thus both reason and affection bear witness to man's immortal nature.

In a sermon preached in ancient Antioch of Pisidia, and preached to a congregation which rejected the gospel, the preachers, Paul and Barnabas, said, "Seeing ye put it from you, and judge yourselves unworthy of everlasting life, lo, we turn to the Gentiles." How many, alas, there are who judge themselves unworthy of everlasting life and order their lives in a way that takes in only the dying pleasures, the fading joys, and the crumbling possessions of this world! But man is too great for that.

> Were I so tall to reach the pole,
>   Or grasp the ocean with my span,
> I must be measured by my soul:
>   The mind's the standard of the man.[2]

A GREATER LIFE

May I ask you, then, about your plan of life? Is it broad enough? Does it take in others as well as yourself? Does it take in eternity as well as time? Is it deep enough? Does it take in only the temporary occupations and the fading joys of the world? or does it take in the powers of the life to come? Is it true enough? Does it take in God's wonderful plan for the salvation of the soul through the shed blood of Christ?

Are you living without prayer, without worship, without the Word of God, without the fellowship of God's Holy Spirit? Is your path unattended by the music of the heavenly voices? Then your plan of life is too narrow, too short, too shallow, too mean, and too small for one who was made in the image of God.

One of the world's greatest scientists, discoverers, and physicians, taking a final leave of his students and of his life's work, summed up all the wisdom he had gathered in the world and all the advice he had to give to the new generation in that sublime and immortal exhortation of

[2] Isaac Watts, *Horae Lyricae*.

John, "Love not the world, neither the things that are in the world, . . . for all that is in the world, the lust of the flesh, and the lust of the eyes, and the pride of life, is not of the Father, but is of the world. And the world passeth away, and the lust thereof: but he that doeth the will of God abideth for ever."

Michelangelo came one day into the studio of Raphael and looked at one of Raphael's early drawings. Then he took a piece of chalk and wrote across the drawing, "Amplius," which means, "Greater," "Larger." Raphael's plan was too cramped and narrow. God looks down on our plan of life today, and knowing what is in man, writes over that plan, "Amplius." Greater! Larger!

VI

"Who told thee that thou wast naked?"
Gen. 3:11

GOD'S CLOTHING

ADAM DID NOT ANSWER. THE ANSWER IS GIVEN IN THE next question of the Almighty, "Hast thou eaten of the tree, whereof I commanded thee that thou shouldest not eat?" That was how Adam knew he was naked.

When he was called out of his hiding place into the presence of God after his fall, the man said, "I heard thy voice in the garden, and I was afraid, because I was naked; and I hid myself." Adam states the consequence of his fall, a sense of nakedness and fear in the presence of God. But God takes him back to the cause of that sense of fear and shame. Their transgression told the man and the woman that they were naked in the presence of each other and naked in the presence of God. Sin is the mother of shame. When the first sin had been committed and their eyes were opened, the man and the woman sought to cover themselves. So man has been doing ever since. What is civilization, in all the length and breadth of its many-colored coat, but a vast and prolonged effort on the part of man to cover his nakedness?

The more man knows, the more wonderful becomes the book of Genesis. The increase of the kingdom of man's knowledge serves only to emphasize by way of contrast the vast range of vision of the man who wrote these

64

pages. The higher man builds the pyramid and tower of his knowledge and his place of observation, the more clearly he sees the altitude upon which the author of Genesis stood. How perennially fresh is the water we draw out of this deep well! What grand thoughts haunt us here!

The commonest facts are sometimes the strangest. Nothing is more ordinary and common and universal than clothing; and yet, when you think of it, what a strange thing a dress or a suit of clothes is! In *Gulliver's Travels* Swift brings his hero to the land of the Houyhnhnms. In this country the horse is the ruling animal. Gulliver takes a position as man-servant to a prominent horse in the community. His master is greatly interested in what Gulliver tells him of the ways and habits of man. One day the Houyhnhnm happens to see Gulliver remove his clothing; and of all the things that he has yet learned about man, that strikes him as the oddest and most extraordinary. Custom has taken away from us the fact of the singularity of clothing; but how strange a fact it is! Man is, on one side of his nature, a creature, an animal, like all the others; and yet, of them all, he is the only one who wears clothes.

CLOTHES AND THE PRE-EMINENCE OF MAN

If you were to go to a world in which there were neither men nor animals, and were asked to explain to some intelligent creature there the difference between men and animals in your own world, you might mention speech and reason and tools. But you sum up the difference completely when you describe it in the terms of clothing.

The chief difference between man and the animal is that man wears clothes.

Various explanations have been given of man's being the only clothed animal. One is that his wearing clothing was due to the climate—that the climate changed; or that when man migrated from a warm climate to a cold climate, he felt the need of artificial covering. But that is not satisfactory, for the same would apply to animals, which have a much more convenient and less expensive way of protecting themselves against the rigors of the climate. Another explanation is that it grew out of man's instinct for decoration—he began to scrawl his pictures on the walls of his cave, and then went a step higher and was pleased to see the difference which the skin of a beast or the feather of a bird made in his own appearance or in the appearance of his companion; thus clothing became permanent; and with the wearing of clothes there finally arose the sense of modesty and shame. As Carlyle puts it in *Sartor Resartus,* "Shame, divine shame, as yet a stranger to the human bosom, arose there mysteriously under clothes, a mystic grove encircled shrine for the holy of man."

But the writer of Genesis, going back to the origin and source of things, tells us that clothing did not come as a result of climate or of man's instinct for decoration, but from his sense of shame. The clothing did not produce the sense of shame, but shame and modesty produced the clothing; and the sense of shame came from man's transgression. Thus clothing marks the dawn of guilt. The true and divine order is this—sin, shame, clothing.

Clothing, or the instinct to cover oneself with clothes, is a fact which declares the separateness and uniqueness

of man's nature. You may trace for me the channels of
the blood as it courses through the veins of a man or a
beast; you may demonstrate that the reflex actions in
certain animals are just the same as in man; you may
stand up against the wall a collection of skeletons and show
how like the highest anthropoid ape's is to that of man;
but until you can bring in a lion wearing shoes, or an
elephant with trousers, or a giraffe with a collar, or a
cow draped in a shawl, I shall not worry about the sim-
ilarity between myself and the beast. The simple fact of
clothing proclaims an unbridgeable gulf.

That man is distinct, peculiar, unique, sacred, in the
essence of his nature is a fact that needs reiteration and
proclamation today. The ethics of the jungle and the code
of the beast are being advanced in some circles as a suit-
able substitute for the Ten Commandments. The highest
good in life is the right to satisfy immediately any and
every natural desire. Hence we must strike the note of
man's moral nature, of his responsibility and accountability
to a higher law—that the highest happiness consists in
obeying the moral law, and that the deepest misery follows
the breaking of that law. If he would be happy, let man
live not as a beast, but as a child of God.

CLOTHES PROCLAIM THE FACT OF
MAN'S FALL AND SIN

This same singularity, clothing, which proclaims and
proves man's separateness and greatness and pre-eminence, also proclaims the fact of his guilt and sin. Clothing
reflects the dawn of guilt. To say that the man and the
woman knew that they were naked is simply another
way of saying that they knew that they were sinners.

Here, then, we catch the first note of that bell of conscience which rings through man's history. When they sinned, they knew that they were naked, and they sought to cover themselves. Conscience had commenced its sublime and mysterious work. Efforts have been made to account for conscience in some natural and evolutionary way—that it was the result of the conflict between the desire of the individual and the desire of the herd, or the group; the man debated which course to follow, and thus arose conscience, his fear when he had done what he wanted to do rather than what the herd or the group wanted to do. Thus conscience, we are told, was the precipitate of habit. There is nothing really moral about it. All right and wrong are but ideas which have gathered about certain conventions or customs. Yet conscience, regardless of such theories and efforts to dispose of her, goes on doing her work, summoning men and women to the bar of her inescapable judgment. When Herod, who had killed John, heard of the works of Jesus, he brushed aside all the explanations and accounts of Jesus and said, "It is John, whom I beheaded: he is risen from the dead." Yes, conscience is an elemental thing in man's nature, forever proclaiming his greatness and also his sinfulness.

> Yet still there whispers the small voice within,
> Heard through Gain's silence, and o'er Glory's din;
> Whatever creed be taught or land be trod,
> Man's conscience is the oracle of God.[1]

Thus it is that every suit of clothes, every milliner's shop, every display window in a department store, is a

[1] Byron, "The Island."

witness to the fact of sin, of conscience, of man's fall, for all clothing goes back to that. This is a definition and an explanation which fits, first of all, the disharmony and internal rebellion of human nature. Man has the appetites and the desires of the animal; but he has other instincts and other desires, and, unlike the animal, he cannot gratify the animal appetites of his nature and think that is the end of it; for he is haunted by the past and threatened by the future. The fact, then, that man is fallen, that his nature today is in disorder, fits human nature as we know it. This explanation of man's condition is in agreement also with the divine remedy of Christianity, which is not a new education, nor the increase of knowledge, nor a further development, but atonement and the washing of regeneration.

Since the days of Adam mankind has tried hard to dispose of the fact that he is a sinner. In his life of Bunyan, Froude pays this tribute to the sense of sin in human society: "Conviction of sin has become a phrase, shallow and ineffective, even in those who use it most sincerely. Yet moral evil is still the cause of nine-tenths of human misery, and it is not easy to measure the value of a man who could prolong among his fellow creatures the sense of the deadly nature of it." The sense of sin is the one restraint and barrier between man and the abyss. It is the foundation upon which the future of the human race must be built.

GOD'S CLOTHING FOR MAN'S NAKEDNESS

There is a school of allegorical interpretation of the Bible which goes to great and unwarranted extremes. In every Old Testament fact or incident or number, in the fittings and colors in tabernacle and temple, in the plagues of Egypt, and in the wilderness wandering, some type or shadow of a Christian fact has been discerned. It is well to be hesitant in our acceptance of such conclusions. But certainly in its use of the origin of clothing the allegorical school did not go far astray. How profound is the truth which is here set forth! Man, when he knew that he was naked, sought to make a covering of his own, and failed. Then God addressed himself to man's condition and made him a covering out of the skins of beasts. To cover his nakedness was not so easy as man had thought; it took the life of an animal. And here we have the figure of the truth that the covering of man's sin and guilt is no simple and easy matter. All man's most elaborate efforts are in vain; all his knowledge, all his art, all his self-righteousness. It takes life and death, even the life and death of Christ, to cover the nakedness of man's sin. "Without shedding of blood is no remission."

Who shall cover the nakedness of man? The scholar answers, "I will clothe him. I will weave for him a garment of knowledge which will cover his nakedness and make him fit to stand before God." And from the loom of knowledge man takes down this garment that has been woven for him and casts it about him. But, alas, when he goes into the presence of God, the beauty of the robe vanishes. It drops in rags about his feet, leaving him naked in the presence of God.

Who will clothe the nakedness of man? "I will do it," says the lawmaker. "I will devise and enact laws to govern his course of life and guide him in what he shall do. If he keeps my laws, he shall come to perfection." From the loom of legislation man takes down the garment that has been woven and casts it about him. But when he goes into the presence of God, the beauty of the garment vanishes, and it drops in rags about his feet.

Who will clothe the nakedness of man? "I will do it," says the artist. "I will teach him to love the beautiful in form and color. I will set before him the matchless creations of Praxiteles and Phidias and Michelangelo. I will let him behold angels rising out of granite, and heavenly spirits out of clay. I will show him the beauty of the mist hanging over the mountains; of the child asleep on its mother's breast; of the wild beast in its desert solitude; of birds sailing beneath the clouds, and ships sailing over the waves. I will open his ears so that he can hear the music of the world and introduce him to the harmony of the universe, in which there is blended the roar of the waves as they break on iron cliffs; the sob of the brokenhearted; the shout of the victor; the lament of the dying; the cry of little children; and the breath of the prayer which goes up to God on the wings of devotion." And from the loom of art man takes down the garment that has been woven for him and casts it about him. But when he goes into the presence of God, lo, the garment shrivels and disappears, and he is left naked.

Who will clothe the nakedness of man? And out of the darkness of Calvary comes a great Voice, "It is finished! I will clothe his nakedness." Here is a garment whose texture and fabric have been designed from before the foundation of the world and wrought out by the eternal counsels of God. The robe is white; but it has been made white through the blood of the Lamb. "These are they which came out of great tribulation, and have washed their robes, and made them white in the blood of the Lamb."

71

The righteousness of Christ is the only garment which can clothe the nakedness of the sinner. Have you put on that garment?

> Nothing in my hand I bring,
> Simply to thy cross I cling;
> Naked, come to thee for dress;
> Helpless, look to thee for grace;
> Foul, I to the fountain fly:
> Wash me, Saviour, or I die! [2]

[2] Toplady, "Rock of Ages."

VII

"In the whale's belly . . ."
Matt. 12:40

A WHALE'S BELLY FOR A PULPIT

JONAH PREACHED THE SHORTEST AND THE GREATEST sermon on record. It was a sermon of just eight words, "Yet forty days, and Nineveh shall be overthrown." That sermon brought the great city of Nineveh to its knees and to repentance, from the king upon his throne to the beggar on the dunghill. Yet that sermon would never have been preached had Jonah himself not repented and prayed unto God out of the belly of the whale. Jesus himself recognized Jonah as a great preacher, for he said that Nineveh repented at the preaching of Jonah, but "a greater than Jonah is here."

The call of God came to Jonah telling him, "Go to Nineveh, that great city, and cry against it; for their wickedness is come up before me." Every time the city of Nineveh is mentioned in the four chapters of Jonah, it is spoken of as a "great" city, "an exceeding great city of three days' journey." That is, it would take three days to walk through and around the city. At this time it was the world's greatest city, built on the bank of the Tigris River, and the capital of the Assyrian Empire. It was a city of architectural magnificence and the center of a vast population. It was also a city of great wickedness and corruption. Long afterward God said through the prophet

Nahum, "I will make thy grave; for thou art vile." Nineveh was as cruel as it was vile, and its path to empire and world dominion was marked by the colossal mounds of the skulls of the slaughtered.

When Jonah received his commission from God to go to Nineveh and cry against it, he disobeyed it and fled from the presence of the Lord. One of the reasons for this flight and disobedience is given in Jonah's own words in the last part of the book. He said that instead of going to Nineveh he fled to Tarshish, because he knew that the Lord was a gracious God, "merciful, slow to anger, and of great kindness, and repentest thee of the evil." Jonah claimed that he foresaw that the end of his preaching would be the repentance of Nineveh, and that God would spare the city, whereas he, like every other patriotic Hebrew, thought the city ought to be destroyed. There was another reason, too, and that was the fact that it was a long and dangerous journey to Nineveh, and to preach such a message in the heart of that city-empire would put Jonah in great peril. The prophets were accustomed to long-distance denunciation of the kingdoms and empires that ruled in their day; but to go in person to one of the capitals of these kingdoms and pronounce its doom, that was something new.

THE FLIGHT OF JONAH

Instead of going to Nineveh, which lay far to the northeast, Jonah went in the very opposite direction. He went to Joppa, which lay on the sea, and took a ship for Tarshish, which was far to the southwest, as far from Nineveh as it was possible for one to go. I can see Jonah down at Joppa, that same Joppa where centuries later on the house-top of Simon the Tanner, Peter had the vision which told him that the gospel was not for the Jews alone, but for all men of all nations. Along the water front, getting ready to sail, or discharging their cargoes, lay many ships. With his face half muffled in his cloak and an anxious, furtive manner about him, Jonah searched for a ship that would carry him far from his native land, far from God's people, and, he hoped, far from God himself. He stopped at one ship and said to one of the sailors, "Mariner, whither bound?"

The sailor answered, "We are bound for Greece."

"That's too near," Jonah said to himself, and passed on to another ship, where he hailed another sailor and said, "Sailor, where does this ship sail?"

The sailor told him, "We sail for Egypt."

Jonah said to himself, "That's too near," and passed on to another ship, where he made the same inquiry and got the answer, "We sail tonight for Cyprus."

"Too near," Jonah said to himself, and passed on to another ship and again made the same inquiry and got the answer, "We sail for Crete."

"Too near," Jonah said to himself, and passed on to another ship, where he hailed a sailor who was rolling a barrel up on deck and said to him, "What is the port of this ship?"

The sailor answered, "We sail tonight for Tarshish."

"Ah," Jonah said to himself, "that is good! Tarshish! Clear over in Spain, at the very end of the world! This is the ship for me!"

Going up the gangplank, Jonah found the mate at a table checking on the cargo. He told the mate where he wanted to go and asked what the fare would be. The mate answered that he would ask the captain. He searched out the captain at the stern of the vessel and said to him, "There's a man come on board who wants to sail with us to Tarshish; but there's something strange about him. I don't like his looks."

The captain said to him, "We don't care anything about his looks. As long as he has the cash, let him sail."

"How much will the fare be?" asked the mate. The captain named the sum, three times the usual fare. The mate went back to Jonah and told him what the fare would be. Jonah thought it was a very high price, but not too high a price if indeed the ship would carry him away from the presence of the Lord.

The sailors on board, busy at their tasks preparatory to sailing, took a look at Jonah, and everyone's opinion was unfavorable. "I'll bet he's a runaway thief," one said.

"More likely a kidnaper," his shipmate answered.

But another said, "He looks more like a murderer to me."

And still another said, "Whoever he is and whatever he is, we'll have no luck on the voyage with that fellow on board."

Jonah, who overheard some of these remarks, felt uneasy; but, pretending indifference, he made his way down the ladder into the hold, where up against the side of the vessel he found some straw and, spreading his cloak over him, lay down. It was a relief to him when he felt the heaving of the ship, letting him know that the vessel had at length sailed. The motion of the ship soon lulled him to sleep. "Jonah was gone down into the sides of the ship; and he lay, and was fast asleep."

JONAH CAST OVERBOARD

For a time all went well with the ship; but after a little the south wind shifted to a wind from the northeast. The stars disappeared. The night was black as Egyptian darkness. The wind howled. The waves smashed against the ship. The sea "wrought, and was tempestuous." The seamen did all they could to fight the gale and make the vessel safe. They probably threw a cable around the waist of the vessel, as the seamen did in Paul's shipwreck, to hold the ship together, and, lowering the sails, took to the oars. Then the valuable cargo was cast into the sea. But all their efforts were in vain; and the ship was driven a helpless hulk before the raging tempest.

The sailors were a composite crew, as is often the case even today on a ship. They represented several nations and religions, and in their fear and distress every sailor cried unto the god whom he had been taught to fear. At length the captain said to the mate, "Where is that fellow who came aboard at Joppa and paid his fare for Tarshish?"

The mate said, "I haven't seen him since he came on board."

"See if you can find him," ordered the captain.

Taking one of the sailors with him, the mate searched in the bow of the vessel, in its waist, under the stern, and under the long boat which was carried for use in an emergency. But there was no sign of Jonah.

"Go below," said the captain, "and see if you can find him there."

After a time the mate appeared on deck again and said, "We found him. He's sound asleep in the side of the vessel on a pile of straw."

The captain then went below and, finding Jonah, awakened him and cried out: "What meanest thou, O sleeper? arise, call upon thy God, if so be that God will think upon us, that we perish not." He was amazed that anyone could sleep during such a storm. Perhaps Jonah, he thought, worshiped a god upon whom no one had yet called.

Up on deck the sailors were certain that someone on board was responsible for the dreadful storm which endangered their lives. Each said to his fellow, "Come, and let us cast lots, that we may know for whose cause this evil is upon us." Watch them as they gathered on the sloping, pitching deck about the brass bowl held by the captain. As the lots were drawn out, conscience began to do its work. Each sailor began to think of his past, as by the light of the swinging lamp he watched the captain draw out the lots. Each one was saying to himself, "Is it I? Is it for my sin that this storm has come upon the ship?" One thought of that merchant he murdered at Tyre. Another thought of the child he kidnaped at Cyprus. Another thought of the Roman officer he murdered at Caesarea. Each man remembered his own sin, and it was with a sigh of relief they saw their names passed over and the lot fall upon Jonah.

The captain then said to Jonah, "What is thine occupation? and whence comest thou? What is thy country? and of what people art thou?" "What is thine occupation?" A most natural question for the captain to ask; but that question pierced Jonah's breast like a sharp sword. "Yes! What is my occupation? I am a prophet of the true God, who made the heavens and the earth; but I have disobeyed his word to go to Nineveh and am

78

fleeing to Tarshish." That question, "What is thine occupation?" brought Jonah to himself and commenced the
great work of repentance in his heart.

Jonah told the captain who he was, and the God whom
he worshiped, and what he had done. Then, going on the
theory that Jonah would know what must be done to
please his God, the captain asked him, "What shall we do
unto thee, that the sea may be calm unto us?"

Jonah answered at once, "Take me up, and cast me
forth into the sea; so shall the sea be calm unto you:
for I know that for my sake this great tempest is upon
you."

The seamen, however, were reluctant to throw Jonah
into the sea, lest they should offend his god, and they
made one more desperate effort with the oars to bring the
ship about and get her to land. But when this failed, they
prayed to Jonah's God, asking him not to lay innocent
blood upon them, and yet not to let them perish because
of Jonah. This done, they took up Jonah in their arms,
carried him to the rail of the pitching vessel, and cast
him into the raging sea. "And the sea ceased from her
raging." The sea was satisfied. The sea, as the agent of
God, upholding his justice and righteousness, said to herself, "It is enough," and ceased from her raging.

"Now the Lord had prepared a great fish to swallow
up Jonah. And Jonah was in the belly of the fish three
days and three nights." I have read learned and labored
discourses dealing with the possibility of a man's being
swallowed by a great fish, and, furthermore, the possibility
of his being kept alive in the fish's belly three days and
three nights. But why discuss such questions as these?
The problem of a man's being able to breathe in the belly

of a great fish, the problem of whether any fish has a
throat big enough to admit the passage of a man's body—
all this is labor wasted. What you are dealing with here
is a miracle. It was a miracle that a man should have survived inside a great fish for three days and three nights,
or for one day and one night, or even for one hour. It
was a miracle, too, that God had the fish at hand to swallow
the recreant prophet. It was a miracle, too, that God spoke
to the fish when it vomited Jonah up on the shore. All this
is miraculous, not natural; contrary to nature, but always
possible with God.

> Admit a God—that mystery supreme!
> That cause uncaused! all other wonders cease:
> Nothing is marvelous for Him to do:
> Deny Him—all is mystery besides.[1]

THE REPENTANCE OF JONAH

In the belly of the whale Jonah repented and prayed.
We have the record of that great prayer in the second
chapter of the book of Jonah. The thoughts and senti-
ments are those which came to Jonah in the midst of that
strange submarine prison; but the final expression of what
he thought and felt was put down afterward, for in the
prayer there is a note of thanksgiving for deliverance.
Many stirring things have been written about experiences
in and under the great waters, such as Jules Verne's
Twenty Thousand Leagues Under the Sea, a prediction
long ago of the submarine. Scientists have gone down
into the waters in a diving bell and have reported what
they saw passing before them in those cold and dark depths

[1] Archbishop Richard C. Trench, *Notes on the Miracles.*

of the sea. But nothing comparable to this record of Jonah was ever written. He says he prayed unto the Lord his God, "out of the fish's belly"; and then changes it to "out of the belly of hell," for to Jonah his prison was indeed the "belly of hell." He said to himself, "I am cast out of thy sight." There is a certain poetic justice, one would say, in that. He had set out to flee from the presence, the sight of the Lord his God; and now it would seem that God has taken him at his word and granted him his desire; for he says, "I am cast out of thy sight." We have his impressions when the fish which swallowed him submerged and plunged down into the depths: "The waters compassed me about . . . ; the depth closed me round about, the weeds were wrapped about my head. I went down to the bottoms of the mountains; the earth with her bars was about me for ever."

In answer to his prayer, when his soul fainted within him and he remembered the Lord, Jonah was cast out upon the dry land. Immediately the word of the Lord came to him the second time: "Arise, go unto Nineveh, that great city, and preach unto it the preaching that I bid thee." This time Jonah at once obeyed. Converted himself, he now set out to convert others. When he reached Nineveh, he began his three-day tour through that great city and around it. Everywhere that he went—past the palaces and the hovels; down the great avenues; to the temples where the false gods were worshiped; in the bazaars, the brothels, the orchards, and the gardens; in the court before the king and the queen; in the barracks of the soldiers; among the boatmen and fishermen on the tawny Tigris— Jonah preached his brief but tremendous eight-word sermon: "Yet forty days, and Nineveh shall be overthrown."

When they heard that sermon, "the people of Nineveh believed God." Everyone, from the king on his throne to the beggar on his dunghill, put on sackcloth and sat in ashes and repented. God saw their repentance and spared the city from the doom and judgment which had been pronounced upon it. If the city, as God said to Jonah, had 120,000 infants who could not discern between their right hand and their left hand, then there must have been a million or more people whom God's mercy spared at that time.

We have heard the great sermon that Jonah preached to Nineveh, and the extraordinary results of that sermon; but Jonah himself is a great sermon, and he preaches a great and timeless sermon to you and me.

WHAT JONAH TELLS US

The first thing Jonah teaches, as illustrated by his life, is that you can never flee from the presence of God; you can never hide from God. Jonah thought he could. He thought that if he could only get to Tarshish, away yonder on the western coast of Spain, clear out of the Mediterranean world, he would be away from the presence of the Lord. But he was greatly mistaken. God followed him to Joppa. God went on that ship bound for Tarshish. God sent out the winds, which are his messengers, to vex the sea. God sent the great fish to swallow Jonah. It is quite likely that Jonah, being a prophet of God, was familiar with the 139th Psalm. If so, "How exactly the truth of that psalm fits me," he must have thought to himself: "Whither shall I go from thy spirit? or whither shall I flee from thy presence? If I ascend up into heaven, thou art there: if I make my bed in hell. behold, thou art there.

If I take the wings of the morning, and dwell in the utter-
most parts of the sea; even there shall thy hand lead me,
and thy right hand shall hold me."

No! It is not possible to flee from the presence of the
Lord. That was a truth discovered at the very beginning
of the creation, when the man and the woman after their
fall heard the voice of the Lord God and hid themselves
from the presence of the Lord God among the trees of the
garden. Do not make this biography of Jonah ancient history, for it is as modern and up-to-date as the last man
and the last woman. Jonah was not the only man with
whom God has had trouble. He has trouble with you and
me, too. As clearly as Jonah ever heard the voice of God
telling him to go to Nineveh, you and I have heard the
voice of God telling us what to do and where to go. The
storm that broke over the Mediterranean that night when
Jonah was on the ship fleeing to Tarshish is a symbol of
the inner storm raised by conscience when you and I disobey God and seek to flee from his presence.

The great sermon of Jonah's life and experience tells
us, in the second place, of the power of prayer and the
blessedness of repentance. By repentance and prayer Jonah
was transformed from a cowardly, renegade prophet to a
true prophet of the Lord, worthy of a place in the sacred
canon, and worthy, too, of the inspired brush of Michelangelo, who made Jonah stand out beyond all other
prophets, sibyls, and apostles in his immortal frescoes on
the ceiling of the Sistine Chapel in the Vatican at Rome.
How great and beautiful and wonderful is repentance!
Under every kind of character, beneath all the needs of
man's heart and the habits of his life, deeper than the
deepest despair, deeper than the blackest sin, lies that

miraculous power of the soul to turn to God and repent. Every soul has within it, under the hand of God, the power to repeat what Jonah did when he repented and prayed unto the Lord out of the belly of the whale, and out of the belly of hell. The repentance of Jonah is a far greater miracle than his being swallowed up and cast out again by the great fish.

Greater, too, as illustrated here in the experience of Jonah, is the power of prayer. From the bottom of the sea, from the belly of hell, as Jonah calls it, we can cry unto God as Jonah did. There were great celebrations and rejoicings when the Atlantic cable was laid in 1858, and the first message was flashed from continent to continent. But what is the Atlantic cable compared with the heavenly cable of prayer, whereby man in a moment of time can communicate with the God of heaven, whether he calls upon him, as Jonah did, out of the belly of hell, or in the private chamber at the close of day confesses his transgressions, thanks God for his mercies, and commends himself unto him for safekeeping through the night?

> But there's a power which man can wield
>   When mortal aid is vain,
>
> .   .   .   .
>
> That power is prayer, which soars on high,
>   Through Jesus, to the throne,
> And moves the hand which moves the world,
>   To bring salvation down.[2]

In the last place, the sermon of Jonah's life tells us the goodness and mercy of God in granting to our souls

[2] John Aikman Wallace.

a second chance. "The word of the Lord came unto Jonah the second time." I never get over being thrilled by that record. "The word of the Lord came unto Jonah the second time"! Jonah certainly did not deserve a second chance. As a prophet of God he was doubly guilty in disobeying God's voice when he spoke to him the first time. Yet God in his goodness gave Jonah a second chance. How many second chances, too, God gives to you and me! What if God spoke once, and then, if we disobeyed, did not speak a second time? What if after we had refused his word, God never sent the Holy Spirit to plead with us again? What if when we sinned, he never let us repent? But God is long-suffering, slow to anger, and plenteous in mercy. Strange that Jonah, who had experienced in such a wonderful way that mercy of God, should have been displeased with God for showing mercy unto Nineveh. But

> There's a wideness in God's mercy,
> Like the wideness of the sea.

Manasseh, the King of Judah, ruled fifty years and filled his reign with wickedness and blasphemy. Yet, when in captivity and suffering he humbled himself and cried unto God, God heard him and gave him a second chance and restored him to his throne.

The word of the Lord came to David as it has come to few men. Yet David answered by a great transgression, breaking in quick succession five of the Ten Commandments—the tenth, "Thou shalt not covet;" the seventh, "Thou shalt not commit adultery;" the eighth, "Thou shalt not steal;" the sixth, "Thou shalt not kill;" and the ninth, "Thou shalt not bear false witness." But when David repented, when he said, "I have sinned," when he said, "Cast me not away from thy presence," God heard him and forgave him and gave him a second chance. Jonah fled from the presence of the Lord, but the word of the Lord came to him the second time; and Jonah obeyed the voice divine.

If you have disobeyed the voice of God, hear him as he speaks a "second time" and gives you a second chance to obey his voice.

VIII

"The bones of Elisha . . ."
II Kings 13:21

THE INFLUENCE OF THE DEAD

ELISHA WAS A GOOD AND GREAT MAN—SO GOOD AND SO great that contact even with his bones in the grave brought the dead to life.

War is the great violator of the honor and desecrator of the sanctity of life. Those things which, until war comes, men hold to be uppermost—the care of the living, respect for the dead, compassion for the suffering, the refinements of the mind and the spirit—are thrown rudely into the background when men engage in the riot and extermination of war. When the "bleeding testament of war" is opened, all other books or testaments, new or old, are closed.

In some nameless village of Israel a man had died. He was decently arrayed for the grave and, after the usual lamentations and mournings, was being carried by his friends to the place of sepulture. They had just arrived at the cemetery when they saw a band of marauding Moabites, who were making their annual foray into the land of the Hebrews. When they saw those ruthless invaders, fear for their own lives mastered their reverence for the dead. They hastily cast the body of their friend into the first sepulcher they came to and made off for their lives. The grave into which they had cast the body happened to be that of the man of God, Elisha, recently dead and buried. As soon as the man touched the bones of Elisha, "he revived, and stood up on his feet."

It is not this extraordinary physical miracle that I desire to emphasize, but what is suggested by it—the perennial moral miracle, the influence of the good after their death upon the living. It is good for us to pause now and then amid the rush and cares of this life and pay a tribute to the memory of the righteous dead. In all cities of the world there are to be seen stately and magnificent monuments and cenotaphs which memorialize the dead of the two World Wars. In front of these monuments and under these triumphal arches have been kindled ever-burning fires, to signify that the memory of the dead shall never pass from the mind of man. But there are things more wonderful and more beautiful than these. They are the invisible monuments, more precious by far than those of stone or marble or bronze or granite, which loving and grateful hearts have reared to the memory of the righteous dead.

In the eleventh book of Wordsworth's *Prelude* there is a line which speaks of the "reanimating influence of memory." Perhaps that is as near as I can come to a definition or statement of my subject—the reanimating influence of memory; and, in particular, the reanimating influence of the memory of the just, for it is forever true, as the wise man said so many ages ago, "the memory of the just is blessed: but the name of the wicked shall rot."

There are times when we are inclined to be depressed, even cynical. We say to ourselves, "What difference will it make what men think of us when we are dead? At the best, or at the worst, in a few years, perhaps in a shorter period, we shall be forgotten. Our names will be sunk in oblivion." But this is only a passing mood. It is not the real verdict of the heart. Man knows that he will be remembered by *someone,* and he has a dread of being remembered for evil rather than for good. Indeed, the emphasis that man places upon the memory of his friends, and upon his own memory when he is gone, is a singular witness to the depth and the power of man's belief in a future life.

Few falser words have ever been spoken than those which Mark Antony is reputed to have uttered over the body of Julius Caesar.

> The evil that men do lives after them;
> The good is oft interred with their bones.

There is a sense, of course, in which evil goes on leaving its blight and shadow even when the man who put it into operation has passed out of this world. But the inference from these words of Shakespeare, that the good men do has but a brief memory and influence compared with the evil men do, is altogether false. If Antony was thinking only of fame and reputation, there may be something in what he said. Fame and reputation are capricious, and may, and oftentimes do, pass over the good in a man's life and preserve the evil; or they may neglect the truly honorable and useful dead and keep fresh in the memory of mankind the names and deeds of those whose lives were infamous. Such fame and memory are altogether uncertain and capricious. Upon what accidents they rest! The destruction or the preservation of some old manuscript; the fancies or prejudices of a historian; the external chances of time or fortune, which leave one name written high and of another leave not a single vestige. There may be men who struggle for that sort of fame, but they pursue a shadow and embrace a mist. In a celebrated passage from *Urn Burial,* Sir Thomas Browne speaks of how Herostratus, who burnt the temple of Diana, lives, while he is almost lost that built it; and how time has spared the epitaph of Hadrian's horse, but confounded that with himself. Then he goes on to say that it is quite possible, and altogether likely, that some of the greatest and most honorable characters in history have never been heard of. It is quite possible that fame and history may exalt those who do not deserve it, while they pass by or neglect the worthy.

But when we come to the memory of the just, there is no doubt about their abiding influence. No accidents of time can destroy that influence. This is the constant miracle. The dead man touched the bones of Elisha and immediately was revived. So we touch, as it were, those who have lived before us and have passed out of this life; and whenever and wherever we touch them, their memory is reviving, reanimating.

There may have been days with you when the Moabites came in like a flood. They may have been in the form of an invasion of sordid motives. You were countenancing things in your life and conduct that once you would have scorned. The golden shields of high resolve and inflexible integrity were gone, and in their place you hung up the shields of brass. Then, suddenly, and with no choosing of your own, you touched the life of one who had lived and died, and who thought of you only in the terms of honor and of truth. That unexpected meeting, that fortunate touch, brought you back to yourself. The body of your dead ideals and forgotten purposes touched the bones of the sainted dead, and you revived and stood up.

Or it may have been when you were drifting upon a lee shore of temptation, and all the considerations of morality and religion and of your own welfare in this world, not to speak of the world to come, were lost sight of. All the anchors which ordinarily hold a man safe had dragged, and, although you may not have realized it at the time, you were drifting rapidly toward the rocks of destruction; then suddenly there flashed on the headlands a warning beacon. It may have been just a single flash, but it was enough to make you realize your peril, the rocks of woe upon which you were driving. That flash saved you. What was it? Or, better, who was it? Father, mother, brother, sister, husband, wife, or child? And where did that sudden light burn, in what kind of a lamp? Perhaps an old portrait, or a faded letter, or a book with love's inscription; but whatever it was and however it came, it was a messenger from God to warn you and to save you. You touched the bones of the godly dead and lived again. One of the most powerful works of Ibsen is his *Rosmersholm,* in which the chief character in the play is kept back from sin by the portraits of his ancestors who look warningly down upon him from the walls of his home.

Or it may have been a day when the stars of faith seemed to have gone out in your heaven. The old divinities were gone; the old beliefs were crumbling; their foundations undermined by doubt or battered by the cruel enginery of life's trials and hardships and sorrows; or their foundations sapped by sin. A gloom was over your soul, and all the birds that sang to you in youth were gone. But in that hour the memory of the just was your salvation. Perhaps you looked upon a portrait which hung on the wall or stood on the desk; and as you looked, the peace and calm of that soul who struggled and overcame through the blood of the Lamb was transferred to you. You opened an old Bible, its pages once smoothed by hands that long had been dust, its verses read by eyes that now behold the King in his beauty; or you sat again in the church where one whom you had loved and honored worshiped; and faith again spoke its grand music of hope and of triumph. In the words of a great hymn—

> Falls on the ear the distant triumph song,
> And arms are strong and hearts are brave again.

In his *Journal,* in the entry for February 28, 1854, soon after his mother's death, Carlyle tells of a vision he had of the old home, Main Hill, with mother, father, and the others getting dressed for church:

They are all gone now, vanished all their poor bits of thrifty clothes, their pious struggling efforts, their little life— it is all away, it has all melted into the still sea, it was rounded with a sleep. Oh, pious mother, kind, good, brave, and truthful soul, as I have ever found, and more than I have elsewhere found in this world, your poor Tom, long out of his school days now, has fallen very lonely, very lame and broken in this pilgrimage of his, and you cannot help him or cheer him any more. But from your grave yonder in Ecclefechan churchyard you bid him trust in God, and that also he will try, if he can understand, and do.

For you and me there are two practical conclusions. In the first place, the importance of an immediate response to the influence of the past and the memory of the just whenever they touch us or speak to us. Great is their power if their voice is obeyed. Harriet Beecher Stowe relates how in that remarkable family of the Beechers, the one irresistible argument and appeal of their father, Lyman Beecher, was his appeal to the memory of their mother. Great is the power of the memory of the just to cleanse and to save.

It may be that I have touched into vibration the mystic chords of memory which lead back to an old home, to a church pew, to some hour of consecration and dedication, or to a mounded grave. I draw the bow at the venture; but if some voice is speaking, if out of the horizon of yesterday some loved face or form has arisen, then whatsoever that voice, whatsoever that memory, says to you, do it; for it is the voice of God.

The other practical conclusion is that we ought to live so as to be worthy of being remembered, so that we shall be remembered for that which is good. Musing once amid the graves in the beautiful Protestant Cemetery at Rome, I came suddenly and unexpectedly upon a stone on which was cut the name of a friend of my college days, a distinguished professor of Latin, who had been at the head of the Latin department of one of our great universities and also the director of the American Academy at Rome. He was a great teacher and a noble man. One writing his memorial quoted words that he himself had once used of Horace: "Friendly, kindly, genial, he has achieved what Tacitus says should be the object of every man's insatiable ambition—he has left a 'happy memory' of himself."

Let us strive so to live that we shall leave behind us a happy and blessed memory of ourselves.

> Only the actions of the just
> Smell sweet and blossom in their dust.[2]

There are only two great societies on earth and in heaven, the noble living and the noble dead. Let us live so as to qualify for those great societies. Live in the faith and fellowship of Jesus Christ, whose memory is forever conquering temptation, relighting the lamp of hope, breaking the bonds of sin, and making the dead to live again. For this very thing, for this eternal influence, that his memory might forever bless mankind, he provided, when, before he suffered and died for us on the cross, he left us the sacrament of his blood and his love, and said, "This do in remembrance of me."

[2] Shirley, *Contention of Ajax and Ulysses.*

IX

"There came a viper."
Acts 28:3

TEMPTATION CONQUERED

It never rains but it pours. One trouble and peril after another came in quick succession upon Paul and his companions. First, a whirlwind which drove their ship up and down in the Mediterranean. Then the beaching of the ship on the rocks, and the perilous landing on the shores of Malta. Delivered from the fury of the sea, they were now drenched with the cold rain which was falling. In order to protect themselves from the inclemency of the weather and to warm their chilled bodies, the survivors of the shipwreck built in a sheltered place a great fire. Paul was not above helping in this enterprise, and with his own hands he brought a bundle of sticks to the fire. As he was about to throw the bundle into the flames, a viper, brought to life by the heat of the fire, suddenly came out of the fagots and fastened itself on the apostle's arm.

When the barbarians saw the serpent on Paul's arm, they exclaimed, "No doubt this man is a murderer, whom, though he hath escaped the sea, yet vengeance suffereth not to live." But Paul shook off the beast into the fire and felt no harm.

This viper, coming suddenly out of the gathered sticks and fastening itself to Paul's arm, may well serve as an illustration of the universality, the secrecy, sublety, and peril of temptation.

THE SOURCE AND DIVERSITIES OF TEMPTATION

The evangelist Luke tells us that at the beginning of Jesus' ministry he was led of the Spirit into the wilderness to be tempted of the devil; and in many other places in the Scriptures the devil, Satan, is declared to be the great author and agent of temptation. But in another great passage on temptation James makes no mention of the devil, but lays the whole responsibility upon man himself, for he says: "Let no man say when he is tempted, I am tempted of God: for God cannot be tempted with evil, neither tempteth he any man: But every man is tempted, when he is drawn away of his own lust, and enticed." Therefore, whatever theories we may hold as to the origin of sin and temptation, the practical fact for us to remember and to deal with is that all men are tempted and that all men have a responsibility in their temptation. If men sin and yield to temptation, it is because they want to. None can exculpate himself on the ground that temptation is too strong for human nature and that in yielding we only follow the natural course of our being. That, as James says, is a reproach to God. The moral world would come down about us in ruins if God permitted temptations which man cannot overcome and out of which there is no escape. "There hath no temptation taken you but such as is common to man: but God is faithful, who will not suffer you to be tempted above that ye are able."

Every man's life is a battlefield, and in this warfare

there is no discharge. On the battlefield of the soul good and evil contend for its mastery and its destiny.

Temptation is as diversified and various as life itself. Almost any occupation or relationship in life has lurking in its bundle a possible viper of temptation. When Paul was engaged in the charitable and important occupation of gathering sticks for the fire to warm himself and his companions, a viper threatened his life. If it had been the most brutal soldier of the ship, or the most hardened and depraved criminal, instead of Paul, who held the bundle of sticks in which the viper lay curled, that would have made no difference to the viper, for a viper is no respecter of persons. Neither is temptation. Nor is temptation any respecter of places, or relationships, or occupations.

The body is a chief channel of temptation, for that comes first which is natural. The viper of sensuality and lust does not hesitate to assail the most gifted and the most honored, that it may drag them into the dust and crucify their happiness and defile their influence for good. See whom it has assailed and whom it has wounded—the heroic and pure-minded Joseph, saved only by flight; the devout and magnanimous David, who was hurled into the mire; the wise and liberal Solomon, whom it seduced in his old age from an early allegiance to wisdom. Surely this temptation is no respecter of persons. Out of the heat of human and personal contact, warmed to life, this viper lifts its venomous head to strike at the worthiest, the most useful, and the most honorable. If a Paul had to say that he kept his body under lest, having preached to others, he himself should become a castaway, then it behooves you and me to say—and to do—"Let him that thinketh he standeth take heed lest he fall." A man who was ruined, and by this temptation in the body, afterward confessed, "I fell because I deemed myself above temptation." Do not repeat his blunder. Remember Hazael, who said, "Is thy servant a dog, that he should do this great thing?" and then went straightway to perform what he thought he could never do.

In the business associations and transactions of life necessary for the commerce and industry of the world there lurks a viper of temptation. How many pitfalls and traps of temptation there are! Acquiescence in an unjust or dishonorable practice will result in gain and extra profit. Or a silence, carefully maintained when truth demands that one should speak, will yield an increase of dividend.

The intellectual life, the world of knowledge, has its own peculiar temptations and dangerous vipers. A father told me of one son, now at a university, who was all at sea as to his religion; of a daughter who had given herself for the work of a missionary in foreign lands, but was now shipwrecked as to her faith. Many other fathers in many other homes could bear a like testimony. The eating of the tree of knowledge has its perils, for suddenly, unexpectedly, the mind may rise in rebellion against God; and only the grace of God is sufficient to quell this state of insurrection. Reason may become a viper which, roused to life by the heat and excitement of knowledge, buries its fangs in the hand of faith.

Years ago an Italian gentleman and scholar was found dead in his chair in his famous library. There was no mark of an attack; there had been no sudden collapse of one of his vital organs; but on his wrist there was the mark of the bite of some venomous insect or serpent. Search was made in the ancient tome which he had been reading. There in this book was found coiled a minute, but deadly, serpent. The world of knowledge has its vipers and its perils.

What we call social life, society, has its own peculiar perils and temptations. How often in society there is sham and imposture, the pretense of a reality not there, or the flippant utterance of falsehood, which pass as social amenities; or the exaltation of pleasure and pride to a place of devotion and worship. Christ said that it was easier for a camel to pass through a needle's eye than for a rich man to get into the kingdom of heaven. He might have added that it was easier for a camel to go through a needle's eye than for a "society woman" to maintain a vital faith and a true relationship with the Lord Jesus Christ.

As for political life, the tragic record of the wounded and the fallen is open, so that all who run may read. For the sake of some temporal advancement or the winning of a campaign, men compromise with evil and excuse themselves on the ground that in politics such things are necessary. How many lies blacken round the corpse of him who gains a name!

Thus the bundle of life, wherever it be gathered, has somewhere sleeping in its fagots, ready to strike, a viper of temptation. The scribes and Pharisees, and others, after hearing what Jesus had to say on the subject of marriage and divorce, concluded that it would be better for a man not to marry at all. After the same manner, men might say that if life is so benetted round with temptations from within, from others, from the Prince of Darkness himself, it would be better not to live at all. Yet Christ in his great prayer for his disciples, and for us today, prayed not that they might be taken out of the world, but that they might be kept from the evil that is in the world. Even with temptation, with its dreadful power to hurt and mar and ruin and darken, life is a great and sacred thing. The very peril of life adds to its greatness. Every new life is like a new creation, like another Garden of Eden history. As Augustine said, "In every man and woman there is an Adam, an Eve, and a serpent."

THE WOUNDS OF TEMPTATION

The viper has a deadly bite. Paul, had he not shaken the beast off into the fire, would have perished. A small viper and a large man; yet one piercing of those fangs, and a deadly injury would have followed. Temptations which are resisted and conquered cannot hurt or harm, nor are they any disgrace. Only the temptation yielded to has power to hurt the soul. Milton has a great passage in *Paradise Lost* in which he describes the convulsion that ran through the whole created world when our first parents fell. The surrender of man anywhere to temptation produces a shock to his whole moral nature. It throws him open to the next assault of temptation and may leave him with a sense of hopelessness and despair in the face of his battle with the tempter.

One bite of a viper was enough to have killed even a Paul. One successful attack of temptation is enough to overthrow, nullify, and cancel a long and carefully established character of rectitude and honor. One moment of temptation can undo years of vigilance and care and toil. However we may lament that fact or think it unfair, we must accept it as a fact of life. It is a tragedy with which we are confronted from day to day. One who had done great service in the Church, and for God and man, had this to say on this very subject:

> I have had some degree of experimental acquaintance with Jesus Christ for almost forty years. I have borne the ministerial character for upwards of twenty-five years. I have been perhaps of some little use in the Church of God, and I have had a greater share of esteem among religious people than I had any reason to expect; yet after all, it is possible for me in one single hour of temptation to blast my character, to ruin my public usefulness, and to render my warmest Christian friends ashamed of owning me.

HOW TO RESIST TEMPTATION

One of the best ways to resist temptation is to avoid the occasion and the places and persons of temptation. If, like Christ, we are driven of the Spirit into the wilderness to be tempted of the devil, that is one thing. But no man ought to go into the wilderness to *hunt* for temptation. There is an old legend of a monk who, when assailed by the devil in a low and immoral theater, asked the devil how he could be so bold as to tempt a servant of the Lord. The devil answered, "What business has a servant of the Lord in my territory?" The command given to the man and the woman was not merely that they should not eat of the tree of the knowledge of good and evil, but that they should not even touch it.

William Jennings Bryan used to tell about a drunkard in his town in Illinois who had been converted and reclaimed to a sober, decent life; but when he rode into town on his horse, he would still tie his horse at the horse rail in front of the tavern. His friends warned

him that it would be wise for him to tie his horse somewhere else, for by tying his horse in front of the saloon
he was entering into the territory of temptation.

When the tempter assailed our Lord in the wilderness,
Christ met him with immediate resistance and denial.
Too often the tempted one begins to dally with temptation. The moment the tempter gets the ear of his victim,
he is on the way to a complete conquest. When the barbarians saw that Paul neither swelled up suddenly nor
fell down dead, they concluded that he was a god; that is,
that he had been miraculously preserved. Perhaps it was
a miracle. Perhaps it was a literal fulfillment of what
Christ said in his last address to his disciples, before he
was taken up into heaven, "They shall take up serpents;
and if they drink any deadly thing, it shall not hurt
them." But this is not a necessary explanation of what
happened. More likely, the serpent was not yet roused to
full vigor and had only wound itself about the arm of
the apostle. Had he delayed a moment, it would have buried
its fangs in his arm, and the deadly venom would have
raced through his body. But the moment he saw the serpent on his arm, Paul shook it off into the fire.

The secret of victory is immediate resistance. To ponder,
to debate, to hesitate, to long for the pleasant fruit of
sin while dreading its bitter fruits, is to fail and to fall.
Balaam, the gifted seer and prophet, who with such stirring eloquence could forecast the future of Israel, when
he was first offered a bribe for cursing Israel, answered
with apparent indignation, "If Balak would give me his
house full of silver and gold, I cannot go beyond the word
of the Lord my God, to do less or more." But from the
history in the narrative we judge that all the while he

was secretly turning over in his mind the opportunities for gain. The fate of Balaam was to be slain in battle against the people of God.

When Paul shook the viper off his arm, he shook it off into the fire. He did not shake it off into the bundle of fagots or upon the ground, where it might strike him again or bury its fangs in some other survivor of the shipwreck. He shook it off into the flame. That particular viper would never again menace the life of Paul or the life of any other man. To resist a temptation today, to say, No! but with a certain tone of reservation in our minds, as if we might give it consideration tomorrow, is to make sure that temptation will return, and return stronger than it was before, because we ourselves are weaker. Although Saul tried to kill himself on the bloody field of Gilboa, the finishing blow was given him by an Amalekite, one of those people whom, contrary to the commandment of God, Saul had spared. You spare your temptation today, shake it off into the bushes or to the ground instead of into the fire, into the flames, where it will be reduced to ashes, and it will come back to hiss and to strike and to curse tomorrow.

Our Lord tells us to watch and to pray. Reason is not the strongest thing in man. We have intuition and perception which warn us of a temptation or evil which lurks in any person, companionship, work, or occupation of life. When so warned, we ought to watch. Watch and pray! No viper ever was able to wound a man on his knees. In one of my churches there was a fine old elder who used to lead in prayer at the Wednesday night meetings. There were certain verses of familiar hymns which he never failed to quote. One of them was this:

103

Satan trembles when he sees
The weakest saint upon his knees.

Not bad poetry; but there is more truth than poetry in it. One of the chief defenses against tempation is to realize that to yield to temptation is not only to injure ourselves, but also to sin against God. The greatest illustration of that in the Bible is the case of Joseph. With most men opportunity results in sin. But in the case of Joseph there was not only opportunity, but also importunity. Day after day he was unavoidably subjected to that terrible temptation. When at length the temptation reached its height, the thing that saved Joseph was the consideration of how, if he yielded, he would sin against the Holy God of his fathers. "How then can I do this great wickedness, and sin against God?"

Conscience is strong, and conscience will ring its bell in the face of evil; but passion is stronger than conscience. Reason is strong, and reason will expostulate with the tempted man and tell him that the thing he so much desires will turn to ashes when he touches it; but passion is stronger than reason. But there is one thing stronger than passion and stronger than reason, and that is the fear of God. Cord after cord with which a man might bind himself to keep himself from going into the arms of temptation will be broken in the transport of his passion and desire. But the fear of God is a cord which never breaks, once it is firmly bound about the soul. "Stand in awe, and sin not." There are two historic utterances of great men in connection with their temptations. One, this cry of Joseph in the house of Potiphar, "How then can I do this great wickedness, and sin against God?"

The other, the cry of David out of the depths after his terrible fall," "Against thee, thee only, have I sinned." Far better that you should utter the cry of Joseph, than that you should be compelled to utter the cry of David.

THE JOY OF OVERCOMING

We have reflected upon the diversity of temptation, the terrible wounds which it inflicts, and ways of resisting it and overcoming it. Now, in conclusion, it is our privilege to think of the joy of overcoming temptation and of the blessing of temptations endured. Temptation has its perils and woes; but temptation overcome has its solid joys and lasting pleasure. "Blessed is the man," said James, "that endureth temptation: for when he is tried, he shall receive the crown of life." Life has no crown to offer like that which it offers to the man who has overcome temptation. There is no wreath of worldly honor, no decoration, no prize, comparable with the crown of glory won by gallantry in the face of the enemy on the battlefield of the soul. The Apocalypse speaks of filthy locusts which came out of the pit to curse the sons of men, and which had crowns of gold upon their heads. Many things which are evil in this world seem to wear a crown of gold; but death is seated on that crown. The crown of life belongs only to the man who has overcome temptation.

With victory comes an inner strength, an unconscious influence for good. Welling up within one is the glad joy that he has been made fit for the fellowship of saints, martyrs, and angels. He can look to the future without a fear, for now he knows that greater is he that is in us— Christ—than he that is in the world. Jesus overcame his temptation. In his graphic and beautiful language Matthew tells us that "then the devil leaveth him, and behold, angels came and ministered unto him." Blessed and glorious angels, still sent forth to minister unto them who overcome temptation and who shall be the heirs of salvation, come now with your unspeakable ministry to wait upon us when we have overcome our temptations!

X

"And Gashmu saith it."

Neh. 6:6

"THEY SAY"

WHEN AARON BURR AT THE END OF HIS LONG LIFE, during which he had tasted the cup of honor and distinction and also drained the dregs of bitterness and humiliation, lay dying in a boarding house at Port Richmond, Staten Island, a friend who was waiting upon him, reporting to him some rumor, commenced by saying, "They say." At that Burr interrupted her and said, "My dear, never use that word. It has broken more hearts than any other."

Very likely Burr's protest and remark had something to do with his own experience. His character, in spite of his great inheritance as a son of the second president of Princeton and as a grandson of one of America's greatest thinkers, Jonathan Edwards, left much to be desired, down to the very end of his life. The sorrows and adversities through which he had passed, especially the death at sea of his beloved daughter Theodosia, which, he said, had severed him from mankind, had softened him, but apparently had not reformed his manner of life. Nevertheless, Burr was probably painted a great deal blacker than he really was. He himself knew the wound that can be inflicted by a careless and ill-considered, "They say," and he was not wrong when he declared that this is a phrase that has broken more hearts than any other. How

107

many friendships it has destroyed, how many incurable wounds it has inflicted, and how many lives it has saddened!

Nehemiah is one of the grandest characters of the Old Testament. Commissioned by Artaxerxes, the king of Persia, to be the governor of Jerusalem and to rebuild its walls, he had returned to Jerusalem with a company of exiles. Nehemiah was grieved and shocked at the ruin into which Jerusalem had fallen. After he had made a midnight ride about the city and a survey of its walls and gates, he called together the leaders of the returned exiles and said to them, "Let us build up the wall of Jerusalem."

As soon, however, as Nehemiah began his work of reconstruction, he encountered malignant opposition from the chieftains of the tribes living in the vincinity of Jerusalem. The leaders among these were Sanballat the Horonite, and Tobiah the Ammonite, and Geshem, or, as he is called elsewhere, Gashmu the Arabian. These men and their followers sought in every way to prevent the building of the wall. First they tried ridicule. In an interview with Nehemiah they mocked at the Jews' efforts to restore their city; they declared that if even a fox went up on the wall, he would break it down. Then they tried the threat of an armed attack. But Nehemiah armed all his workers with the sword. Everyone who worked with a trowel had a sword girded on his thigh.

Then the enemies of Nehemiah tried to entice him into a supposedly friendly conference, where they could assassinate him. As a last resort they tried to frighten him from his noble task by a slanderous report. They came to him with an open, unsealed letter, the inference being that everyone was aware of its contents. Just who the author of it was is not given. In the letter was this statement: "It is reported among the heathen, and Gashmu saith it, that thou and the Jews think to rebel: for which cause thou buildest the wall, that thou mayest be their king, according to these words."

This was a dangerous charge, and a dangerous rumor to be afloat, that the purpose of Nehemiah in rebuilding the walls and defenses of Jerusalem was to set himself up as king. But Nehemiah, instead of being frightened by this slander, denied it and denounced it to Sanballat, asked God to give him strength for his task, and went on with his work until the walls were completed. "So built we the wall."

Sanballat and Tobiah, Ezra and Zechariah, and Nehemiah himself, save for the inspiring memory he left behind him, are dead and gone long ago. But this man Gashmu, strangely enough, the author of "They say," is still alive. You will find him in ancient Jerusalem and in modern Pittsburgh. He belongs to all races and nations, and speaks all languages. He has other names, too, such as, "They tell me," "Have you heard it?" "Do you think it can be true?" "Don't tell anyone else, but"—Yet he is always hard to locate. His name never appears in the telephone book, and if you search for him at his last reported address, it will be found that he has always moved elsewhere.

Gashmu, then, is the sign and symbol of the talebearer, the defamer, the detractor, and the slanderer. What he did, or tried to do, in ancient Jerusalem in the day of Nehemiah, and what he does, or tries to do, in this day and generation, brings up the whole subject of loose gossip, vague rumor, and malicious defamation. In speaking of this sin let us see, first of all, how Gashmu's report origi-

nates and spreads; and second, the great difficulty of re-
calling it and righting the wrong done by a carelessly or
maliciously spoken "They say"; and in the third place,
the attitude of the Christian man, either as the object
and victim of Gashmu's "They say" or as the man to
whom Gashmu speaks.

HOW AN EVIL REPORT ORIGINATES
AND SPREADS

The evil report is sometimes conceived out of pure
malice. There was a fabled creature, the Ichneumon, which
made it its business to seek out and destroy the eggs of
the crocodile, but which never ate the eggs which it thus
destroyed. So, although we do not like to admit it, there
are those who, without any motive save that of the natural
wickedness of fallen human nature, originate and set in
circulation an evil tale concerning their neighbor. These
are they of whom the Bible speaks as men who love
and make a lie. They are the wicked who "bend their
bow in darkness, and under whose tongue is the poison
of asps." They "sneer at the just, contemn the brave, and
blacken goodness in the grave."

One of the old fables relates how on the occasion of a
triumphant procession of wickedness in hell, the snake and
the slanderer refused to yield precedence one to the other
and began a loud and noisy dispute as to which of them
had the right to go first, for in the infernal regions
the rule is that he takes precedence who has done most
harm to mankind. In this angry dispute the slanderer
showed his tongue to the snake and boasted of the evil
he had done with it, while the snake showed his fangs
to the slanderer and boasted of those he had slain with

his venom. He hissed out to the slanderer that he would not put up with his affront in claiming precedence, and was actually leaving the slanderer behind in the procession. Whereupon Satan took the slanderer's part and, rebuking the snake, drove him back, saying to him: "I recognize your great merit; yet I justly assign precedence to the slanderer. You are excessively venomous, and dangerous in the extreme to everything which is near you. Your sting is fatal, and, which is no merit, you sting without provocation. But there is one thing which you cannot do; you cannot wound from afar like the deadly tongue of a slanderer, from whom there is no escape, even though mountains or oceans intervene. It is clear, then, that the slanderer is more deadly than you are. To him, therefore, belongs the pre-eminence. Give place to him, and in the future behave more quietly."

There are, alas, those who "love and make a lie." But far greater injury is wrought by those who ignorantly, lightly, and carelessly pass on an unfavorable report. The original liar and defamer would have little success in his despicable enterprise were it not for the aid he gets from those who put into circulation the evil word that he first has coined. This is easily, carelessly, but never innocently, done. How easy it is to have upon our lips, or to give heed to it upon the lips of others, such a phrase as this, "They say," "They tell me," "I do not believe it, but—," "Do not tell anyone else—but," "Someone said to me," "This is just between you and me." Thus men become allies of the defamer and permit themselves to become a link in the sewer of detraction and slander.

The ease with which this work of Gashmu is done is due to a lamentable, but undeniable, tendency in human nature to take delight in hearing what is discreditable to another. One of the patent proofs of the fall of man is this terrible inclination of mankind in general; and, on the other hand, one of the proofs of a real conversion and of a regenerate heart is a refusal to take up an evil report against a fellow man. As Paul put it in his beautiful way, "Love thinketh no evil; rejoiceth not in iniquity." But the sad fact is that there are still a vast multitude who delight to think evil and who rejoice in iniquity. Because this is so, Gashmu's "They say" has a large part and place in human life and is the source and fountain of much woe and misery and sorrow.

Those who originate or spread evil reports can also tell the truth with an overstatement or an understatement which throws out a false inference and a dangerous innuendo. What is required, therefore, in speech is not only accuracy, but loyalty; accuracy in words and loyalty in spirit. For example, on a sailing vessel the mate of the ship, yielding to a temptation, became drunk. He had never before been in such a state. The captain entered in the log of the ship the record for the day, "Mate drunk today." When the mate read this entry, he implored the captain to take it out of the record, saying that when it was read by the owners of the ship, it would cost him his post, and the captain well knew that this was his first offense. But the obdurate captain refused to change the record, and he said to the mate, "This is the fact, and into the log it goes." Some days afterward the mate was keeping the log, and, after he had given the latitude and longitude, the run for the day, the wind and the sea, he made this entry, "Captain sober today." The indignant captain protested when he read the record, declaring that it would leave an altogether false impression in the minds of the owners of the vessel, as if it were an unusual thing for him to be sober. But the mate answered as the captain had answered him, "This is the fact, and into the log it goes." This is a good example of how by an accuracy of statement, but by misrepresentation of circumstances, one can injure the character of another.

THE DIFFICULTY OF RECALLING "THEY SAY"

One of the most difficult things in the world is to re-call a careless "They say" or undo the wrong that has been done by it. When one has lightly or carelessly lent himself by some ill-considered word to a plot to damage a fellow man, it will be very difficult, sometimes impossi-ble, for him to withdraw from that conspiracy.

There is, first of all, the solemn and arresting fact that we form an estimate of others through some careless, or even malicious, word or report concerning them. "It is re-ported . . . , and Gashmu saith." Thus an altogether false impression is formed of people, not through real contact with them or knowledge of them, but through loose rumor and vague report.

The slanderer's sin is the meanest and most cowardly of all, for even when there is not the slightest basis of fact or truth, the mere charge or report of evil casts a shadow over men's characters; and an impression is made which it may be impossible to blot out, just as when you scatter feathers on a street when the wind is blowing, and then, when the wind has subsided, go out and try to find the feathers again. How many hearts are broken by the unchristian use of the tongue! In a California cemetery under the shadow of the mountains I came upon a grave in the sand with a strange epitaph on it. The first name of the deceased was given, the date of her birth and death, and then these words:

> Who died of grief
> Caused by a neighbor.
> She rests now in peace.

Perhaps what that epitaph says is true, and the woman whose dust sleeps there was wounded to death by the tongue of a whisperer and a slanderer. Perhaps what is written there is not true; and in that case the slanderer made use of the dead to slander some living person. But in either case that lonely grave with that strange epitaph is a witness to the power of death that is in the tongue. It is an interesting fact that although in the Bible the sin of lying is repeatedly denounced and forbidden, the only kind of lying that is specifically forbidden is lying about others.

THE ATTITUDE OF THE CHRISTIAN MAN

When a Christian man is the victim of Gashmu and his tribe, the best course for him to follow is that of Nehemiah. A man of smaller caliber would have been frightened away from his noble undertaking, the building of the walls of Jerusalem, by the reported rumor that he had treasonable purposes. But Nehemiah calmly, but emphatically, denounced the slander, prayed to God to strengthen him, and went courageously on with his work until the wall went up. Over the portals of one of the colleges of Edinburgh University are cut these significant words, "They say. What do they say? Let them say." This

114

is the wise attitude of a good man. The main thing, after all, is not what *they* say, but what *conscience* says, and what God says.

In his lines on hope, Cowper, under the name of Leuconomus, eulogizes the great preacher Whitefield, and describes his attitude toward detractors and slanderers:

> Assail'd by scandal and the tongue of strife,
> His only answer was a blameless life,
> And he that forged and he that threw the dart
> Had each a brother's interest in his heart.

But what of the Christian man to whom Gashmu comes with his "They say"? Hannah More used to say to anyone who came with a discreditable report about another, "Very well. Let us go together and ask him about it." She records that her invitation was never accepted.

The Christian ideal is to think no evil and speak no evil, but to deal with others and speak of others as you would like them to speak of you. If you feel that you must render an evil report, say it to God; and then at once you will find it impossible to say it to others. The grand Old Testament description of the godly man still stands: "Who shall abide in thy tabernacle? who shall dwell in thy holy hill? He that walketh uprightly, and worketh righteousness, and speaketh the truth in his heart. He that backbiteth not with his tongue, nor doeth evil to his neighbour, nor taketh up a reproach against his neighbour."

Always the Christian man, when he is tempted either to pass on an evil report or to start one himself, will remember his own great need of forgiveness and of cleansing; and he will say to himself and to God:

115

> Teach me to feel another's woe,
> To hide the fault I see;
> That mercy I to others show,
> That mercy show to me.[1]

The cure for the evil tongue is a true conversion, and the love of Christ in our hearts. "Set a watch, O Lord, before my mouth; keep the door of my lips."

[1] Pope, "Universal Prayer."

XI

"Michael the archangel, when contending
with the devil he disputed about the body
of Moses . . ."   Jude 9

THE BATTLE FOR MAN'S SOUL

WHEN CHARLES SPURGEON WAS ONCE BEING SHOWN
through the library of Trinity College, Cambridge, he
stopped to admire a bust of Byron. The librarian said to
him, "Stand here, sir, and look at it."

Spurgeon took the position indicated and, looking upon
the bust, remarked, "What an intellectual countenance!
What a grand genius!"

"Come, now," said the librarian, "and look at it from
this side."

Spurgeon changed his position and, looking on the
statue from that viewpoint, exclaimed, "What a demon!
There stands a man who could defy the Deity." He asked
the librarian if the sculptor had secured this effect de-
signedly.

"Yes," he replied, "he wished to picture the two characters, the two persons—the great, the grand, the almost
supergenius that he possessed; and yet the enormous mass
of sin that was in his soul."

Strange, and in many ways forbidding, is this brief
one-chapter book of Jude. As scowling gargoyles look men-
acingly down upon him who enters one of the old cathedrals, so this mysterious book is like a gargoyle at the

golden gate which opens into the glorious cathedral of the Apocalypse of John, with its grand harmonies, its voices like the sound of many waters, its sea of glass mingled with fire, and its great white throne. Nowhere else in the Bible do we come upon such volcanic judgments, such overwhelming condemnation, as confront us in the Epistle of Jude. One might liken it to the enraged ocean breaking upon a rocky barrier and then retreating with sullen roar, or to a summer hurricane which sweeps over smiling fields and peaceful hamlets with the besom of destruction, or to a storm of thunder and lightning at midnight, illuminating the heavens and making the earth shake with the flash of its artillery.

What a book! Here we behold the fall of the angels and contemplate their doom as, without a Redeemer, they await, reserved in everlasting chains in darkness, the judgment of the great day. Here burn the flames of Sodom and Gomorrah, whose citizens were consumed for their unnatural crimes. Here Cain goes guiltily out from the presence of the Lord with a brand upon his brow, and here the Judge of all the earth comes in the clouds with ten thousand of his saints to execute judgment upon all that are ungodly. All that is tragic and terrible in the history of revelation and in the destiny of the universe is set forth in forbidding array in this brief but tremendous epistle.

The letter is a blast on the trumpet against the evil and the evil men which were threatening the Church. These are enemies of "the faith which was once delivered unto the saints." False in their doctrine, they are corrupt and unspeakable in their morals. To the exhortations and warnings of the Church they return scoffing and irreverent answers. To describe their unbounded license and arrogance the inspired writer declares that they speak evil of dignities and rail at the truth; whereas even Michael, the great archangel, when in dispute with the devil over the the body of Moses, did not bring against him a railing accusation, but said, "The Lord rebuke thee." Michael's reserve was perhaps a tribute to the former state of Satan when he was still an unfallen spirit of God. Although Satan is now fallen and in rebellion against God, the great angel Michael, once his comrade before God's throne, remembers Satan's former estate and pays tribute to it. In contrast with his attitude toward the prince of the kingdom of wickedness, these evil men, against whom this epistle is directed, dare to treat with scorn and contempt the acknowledged teachers and apostles of the Church of Christ.

Before we come to our main proposition, there is a by-product of truth in this reference, and that is, that the friends and advocates of the truth do not need to depend upon abuse or rash anger in their encounter with the teachers and representatives of error. The truth needs no such weapons for its defense. Better the calm dignity and confidence of Michael, who said to the devil, "The Lord rebuke thee." It is well to remember that, while it is our duty to expose and denounce and condemn error, the pronouncement of judgment belongs not to man but to God.

Of this strange encounter between a fallen and an unfallen prince of heaven we have no record save this brief and cryptic allusion. As for the body of Moses, all we are told is that, having viewed the Promised Land in the distance, Moses died and was buried "in the land of Moab, over against Beth-peor," and "no man knoweth of his sepulchre unto this day."

> By Nebo's lonely mountain,
>   On this side Jordan's wave,
> In a vale in the land of Moab
>   There lies a lonely grave;
> And no man knows that sepulcher
>   And no man saw it e'er;
> For the angels of God upturn'd the sod
>   And laid the dead man there.[1]

THE CONFLICT OF GOOD AND EVIL IN THE WORLD

Why should Michael and the devil dispute over the body of Moses? Why did the devil want it anyway? Some have conjectured that the language of the epistle here is figurative, and that by the body of Moses is meant the Jewish church, just as we call the Christian church the "body of Christ." Again, it has been suggested that the devil wanted to prevent the secret burial of Moses, so that his tomb might become a place of worship for the children of Israel and thus lead them into idolatry. But all this is mere surmise. Certainly the author refers to the incident as a bit of Hebrew history, or tradition, with which his readers were thoroughly familiar. We shall waste no time in the discussion of the possible historical background, but come at once to the truth for which it is a remarkable and striking setting and illustration; namely, the ceaseless struggle between good and evil in the heart of man for the dominion of the world. As the body of Moses was the

[1] Cecil Frances Alexander, "The Burial of Moses."

subject and object of a dispute between the great arch-angel and the fallen prince of heaven, so the soul of man is a battleground where clash the powers of light and dark-ness, good and evil, Michael and the devil, heaven and hell.

The fact of this conflict is the key to human nature and human history. At the very beginning, after the fall of man, the history of the world was made the judgment of the world when God said, "I will put enmity between thee and the woman, and between thy seed and her seed." That hatred and enmity implanted at the beginning is mutual, implacable, and everlasting. The first view we have of man shows him standing on a battlefield. He is addressed by two principles of conduct—God said; the tempter said. All the struggles of history, the battles be-tween freedom and tyranny, good government and bad government, religion and anarchy, purity and licentious-ness, are but echoes of this struggle on the battlefield of man's own heart.

It is this conflict which explains what sometimes per-plexes us and troubles us, the way in which good causes and good works become infected with the cancer of evil. As Faber put it in his famous hymn,

> Ill masters good, good seems to change
> To ill with greatest ease;
> And, worst of all, the good with good
> Is at cross purposes.

How often we see this! The government which has been set up for man's protection and happiness sometimes be-comes such an enemy of man that the best thing that can happen is its destruction. Science and education are a double-edged sword and can be turned, and have been turned, against the welfare of mankind; and what is more evident than the way in which religion has been invaded by superstition, worldliness, and corruption, so that wherever man builds a church, the devil builds a chapel? Wherever the spirit of mankind moves out with banners and trumpets on the march of progress, there marches ever on its flank the army of the powers of evil. It is this which explains the corruption of the good, and the malignity and persistence, the revirescence of evil in the world.

Paul struck the true and grand note when he said, exhorting the Christian disciples to courage and steadfastness in their battle with temptation and evil, that we "wrestle not against flesh and blood, but against principalities, against powers, against the rulers of the darkness of this world." Our battle is not with evil institutions, such as slavery, or the liquor evil; but with something deeper, darker, more potent, and invisible. You may destroy and overthrow a bad government; you may outlaw a wicked business or institution; but you have not killed the evil principle which animated the body in which it was for a time incarnated. We do not believe in the reincarnation of souls, but we certainly do believe in the reincarnation of evil in the world.

In *The Four Horsemen of the Apocalypse,* a book widely read during World War I, the young friend of the Russian thinker and prophet was jubilant because he thought he saw the downfall of the enemies of righteousness and the imminent overthrow of all the confederated forces of darkness and sin in the world. But the Russian prophet calmed his enthusiasm by his sad but true observation, borrowed from another great vision of the Apocalypse, the beast which emerged out of the abyss with his deadly wound healed: "No; the beast does not die. He is the eternal companion of man. He hides, spouting blood for sixty or a hundred years; but eventually he reappears."

What Jude does for us, then, in this strange book of his is to roll back, as it were, the curtain of our horizon and permit us a momentary glimpse of the extent and range of this battle between good and evil. Its territory is as vast as the universe; its duration as long as time; its theater, the visible and the invisible worlds.

The fact of this struggle helps us to understand what is going on in the world, and with such an understanding we shall not be cast down or dismayed when we see evil, routed and vanquished in one form, returning in some new institution, and sometimes in a much worse form, just as the evicted devil of our Lord's parable, returning to his house, brought with him seven spirits worse than himself.

THE CONFLICT IN OUR SOUL

But, in a more personal aspect, this truth is instructive and helpful for us in our own lives. If we are sometimes a mystery to ourselves, as, no doubt, we often are to others, this is the secret and explanation of it. Victor Hugo in one of his poems wrote, "I feel two worlds struggling within me." I remember seeing once a sculpture by Carpenter which illustrated this saying. Out of a central block of marble emerge two persons, or personalities; the one, intellectual, refined, spiritual, desperately struggling to get free; the other, of the earth, earthy, animal, sensual, cruel. There in the sculptor's thought and creation is expressed what goes on beneath every human breast. Over and over again the master artists of the Bible permit us to view such a sculpture.

In beautiful language Balaam salutes the future of Israel and longs for the death of the righteous, while coveting the gold which he could have as a reward for cursing them. Judas hears the word of Christ, "Follow me," and follows him, but only to betray him for thirty pieces of silver; and yet, after he has betrayed him, Judas is so stricken with remorse that he goes out and hangs himself. Pilate at once recognizes Jesus as a just man and strives to save himself from the guilt of crucifying him; but when he hears someone shout, "Thou art not Caesar's friend," for the sake of his high place and office Pilate hands Christ over to be crucified. Peter avows that he will never forsake Christ, and in the Garden of Gethsemane he seems to make good that vow when he fearlessly draws his sword and cuts off the ear of the assailant of his Lord. Yet, before the night has passed, he has denied with an oath that he ever knew him.

Men have sometimes discussed the question, of whether, when Paul spoke of the fierce conflict that was going on within his breast, the war between the law of the mind and the law of sin, he was referring to the struggles of a regenerate or an unregenerate man, the natural or the Christian man. Is it autobiographic? Or, when Paul says "I" here, does he mean unregenerate human nature? However that may be, there is no doubt that Paul's description of the struggle that went on in his breast is one which fits us all. We are born on a battlefield, and from that warfare "there is no discharge."

When we enter upon the Christian life, we are not set free from that conflict. To imagine so would be like telling a soldier who has enlisted in a regiment for a war that now, having put his name down on the muster roll of the company or regiment, he can lay by his sword and dispense with his rifle. It is when we really enlist in the Christian life and on the side of Christ that the conflict becomes intense, vivid, grim. When Jesus made his appearance in the flesh as the Son of God and the Son of man, there was a furious outbreak on the part of the demons, for they recognized the threat to their kingdom in the advent of Christ. When a man really makes an effort to follow Christ, then the battle commences. "Through much tribulation," said the greatest of all veterans in this ageless war, "we must enter into the kingdom of God." There is no other path.

The remembrance of the fact that this conflict is everywhere going on is of a nature not only to humble us and warn us, but also to fill us with the spirit of prayer and sympathy for others. If we could know the burdens, handicaps, thorns in the flesh, trials, sorrows, invisible struggles, of our fellows in this world, a wave of compassion would surely sweep over us all.

But whether we sympathize with one another or not, or remember our common battles and struggles as we ought to or not, there is One who does know our battles and who sympathizes with our struggles. It is he, the great Captain of our salvation. He, too, was a soldier in this war, and in it received many cruel and painful wounds. Himself having suffered, himself having fought, he is able to help you and me in our own conflict. He is not a great high priest, a distant, remote, and austere

Captain who with cold indifference observes our battle, its daily ebb and flow, but one who fights by our side and rejoices in our victories. Put your faith in him. Over and over again it has been proved that in the time of danger and peril a whispered prayer to him, the very thought of his Cross and of his love, yes, the very mention of his name, has been a refuge from evil and a very present help in the time of trouble.

Jude is indeed a strange book, full of difficult allusions, flashing with lightnings, and reverberating with the thunders of judgment upon fallen angels and fallen men. But that is not all there is to this book. As a stormy day sometimes comes to a close with a beautiful sunset, so this brief and stormy book comes to a conclusion with one of the grandest and most precious of all the promises and sayings of God's Word. It is this: "Now unto him that is able to keep you from falling, and to present you faultless before the presence of his glory with exceeding joy, to the only wise God our Saviour, be glory and majesty, dominion and power, both now and ever. Amen."

XII

"Send us into the swine."
Mark 5:12

THE DEGRADATION OF SIN

STANDING ON THE WESTERN SHORE NEAR TIBERIAS, ONE looks across the beautiful and placid Lake of Galilee to the stern and barren coast of Gadara. In strange contrast with the beauty of the lake, which is forever associated with our Lord, no coast could be more melancholy or forbidding. The mountain country to the east of Galilee was certainly a fit stage for the strange drama of the devil-possessed maniac and the swine.

After a day's teaching at Capernaum Jesus was on his way to the other side of the lake. He was seeking quiet and rest after the labors and the excitement of the day. In the stern of the boat he soon fell asleep upon the pillow; and while he slept, one of those sudden storms of wind to which the lake is subject came rushing down from the direction of Hermon, and the boat was tossed in the waves. Accustomed though they were to the treacherous storms of Galilee, these hardy fishermen despaired of their lives and, arousing the sleeping Christ, asked him if he cared not that they perished. Standing up in the boat, Jesus rebuked the wind and the waves, and there was a great calm. The disciples were amazed, and they feared, saying one to another, "What manner of man is this, that even the wind and the sea obey him?" But they were to see an even greater miracle. They were to see Christ rebuke and quell not only the storm that swept over Galilee, but also one of those more violent storms and convulsions which sweep the souls of men.

THE DEMONS CAST OUT

The country where Christ landed was uninhabited, save for one wretched and terrible inhabitant. His home was in a nearby village. There he had lived with his family and his neighbors in peace and happiness. But one day he began to show signs of insanity; his actions were queer, his mind was clouded, his suppositions were false. What is insanity? Who knows? Can any alienist tell us? We see its effects; but what is it? Before we dismiss the demons as just a figure of speech, it is well to be sure that we know what insanity is.

In the village everyone began to fear and avoid this man. His children and his wife dwelt with him in daily dread. When he became violent, the neighbors sought to bind him with fetters and chains; but, with the super-human strength and energy of the maniac, he broke his chains as Samson did the green withes with which Delilah had bound him. Then he was driven out of the village altogether and took up his abode among the tombs on this lonely and bleak Gadarene coast. Travelers and fishermen passing by that coast could sometimes hear, by day or night, his loud roarings, and now and then they caught a glimpse of the naked and demented hermit, his body covered with self-inflicted wounds, a fearful monument to the fall of man and the power of Satan.

As soon as the disciples' ship grounded on the shore, the wild man ran down to meet them, to see who it was that dared thus to invade his solitary kingdom. But even at a distance the evil spirit, or spirits, within him recognized Jesus and did obeisance to him. It is an impressive fact that the evil spirits who appear in the New Testament never make a mistake as to the Person of Christ. That mistake is reserved for the unbelief of man. This evil spirit, as soon as he saw Christ, worshiped him and cried out, "What have I to do with thee, Jesus, thou Son of the most high God? I adjure thee by God, that thou torment me not."

When the devil-possessed man came near to Jesus, Jesus said to him, "What is thy name?" The mention of a name will sometimes recall the excited and unbalanced man to himself. Perhaps that was the purpose of Christ when he said to this fearful creature, "What is thy name?" It is a beautiful and solemn truth, too, that even the most unfortunate and most degraded has a name, a personality, distinct forever from every other personality, angel, man, or devil. What is thy name? While the bewildered man groped in the chambers of memory and reason for his name, the demon within him answered, "My name is Legion: for we are many."

The command of Christ was: "Come out of the man, thou unclean spirit." The whole mission and message of Christ is summed up in that command to the unclean spirit, spoken there on Gadara's grim shore. Christ comes to expel the evil spirit from humanity and leave the world clothed and in its right mind. This was a command that no demon or angel or man, dead or alive, has the power to disobey. The demon came out of him forthwith and left the man quiet, calm, sane. The wild, distorted features relaxed and became human and rational again. The roar-

129

ing voice was silent. Perhaps tears of relief flowed down
his cheeks. Reason again ascended her throne in the poor
man's life. Jesus, or one of the disciples, handed him a
garment with which to cover his nakedness. He stood
before them now as rational and sensible as any of the
disciples, "clothed, and in his right mind."

When Jesus was about to depart, the man whom he
had thus delivered came down to the boat and besought
him to let him go with him. This request may have been
prompted by gratitude, or perhaps by a natural dread and
fear lest the demons should again assail him. And what
a beautiful request it was! What if all who unite with the
Church had the same earnest desire to be with Jesus that
this man had? But instead of permitting the man to go
with him, Jesus advised him to go back to his village and
to tell his friends and his family what great things the
Lord had done for him, and what compassion he had
shown him. So the man started back to his village. Seeing him at a distance, shepherds who were out with their
sheep and goats hastily drove their flocks to shelter in
the rocky folds and prepared to defend themselves. The
man sadly observed their flight and vainly signaled them
that now there was no occasion for fear, and that both
they and their flocks were safe from his violence.

At length he drew near to his village. Mothers, seeing
him approach, gathered their children about them and
hurried them into the houses, where doors and windows
were bolted and barred. Only the snarling and unfriend-
ly dogs were left to welcome him. But his little daughter,
looking anxiously out the window, called to her mother,
"Mother! It is father! But he is not the same! He has his
clothes on! There's no blood on his face! He's not roar-

ing and cursing, and instead of leaping over the walls and dykes, he is walking steadily up the street!" Then the mother and the other children came and looked timidly out the window; and, sure enough, there he was, the husband and father, "clothed, and in his right mind." He was about to knock on the door, to tell them that now they need have no fear, when the door was flung open, and his wife and children welcomed him home with their embraces and their kisses. Then all down the street, doors began to open, and eager and curious neighbors began to crowd about the house to express their wonder and amazement at what Jesus has done.

THE DEGRADATION OF SIN

But what of the devils? Homeless now and unwilling to leave the country, they besought Jesus that he would not send them out of the country. Seeing a herd of two thousand swine feeding on the cliffs, they besought him saying, "Send us into the swine." Into the swine, therefore, they went, and the swine, disturbed and terrified, ran violently down a steep place and fell over the cliff into the sea. And there the two thousand swine and the legion of devils disappeared.

What a prayer! "Send us into the swine." When he had been healed, the man whom hitherto they had tenanted prayed that Jesus would take him with him. But these unclean spirits made a different prayer. "Send us into the swine." This marked the last stage in their decline and degradation. The devils and evil spirits had once been angels, but they had rebelled against God. That was the first decline. Then they had entered into men to trouble and curse humanity. Now they asked permission to enter

131

into the swine. From angels down to swine! That marked the course of their fearful decline and fall. The petition and history of these demons is an illustration of the downward tendency of sin and the degrading and deteriorative effect of evil in one's life. Sin always works from a higher to a lower level.

You and I deal with men in life, not with demons or swine; and yet in men, alas, we often mark the same kind of decline, and hear even from human lips what is, in substance, the same kind of a request, "Send us into the swine." There was the lost son. He started with a good home, good environment, good opportunity, godly parents. Then he began to ask to get away from his own home. He said to his father, "Give me the portion of goods that falleth to me." From that home he went to the city, with its lights and excitement, and wasted his substance in riotous living. Farther and farther away from his home he went, lower and lower he sank, until we find him a companion of the swine, "and he would fain have filled his belly with the husks that the swine did eat."

When you think of it, what a tragedy there was in the history of these demons! Once they were spirits ever bright and fair at God's right hand, but now were eagerly asking to dwell in swine. The inhabitants of the heaven of heavens wanted to take up their abode in the beast that wallows in the mire! It was not an immediate and sudden transition and decline, but gradual, made by stages; first angels, then men, then swine. So it is with men. The decline is gradual, but certain. Could any of these evil spirits who stampeded the swine into the sea have identified himself with one of those stainless and mighty spirits who once dwelt at God's right hand, a spirit who once asked of the Eternal One for

132

the honor of doing his will and for the light of his countenance, but whose prayer now is, "Send me into the swine"?

THE SECRET PROGRESS OF SIN

Men can go far in moral and spiritual decline without realizing it, just as Samson "wist not that the Lord was departed from him." It is as if another self had been evolved and created. In one of his strange but powerful tales [1] Robert Louis Stevenson tells of a man who has committed a murder. After the fatal blow is struck, the man is startled by an apparition who talks with him and expostulates with him. It proves to be none other than his former self, and this former self traces the course of his decline, how he has slipped from one level to another and now has committed a crime the very thought of which would once have shocked him and horrified him.

The terrible petition of those evil spirits once in the service of God reveals the destructive and progressive effect of yielding to temptation and sin. The soul slowly loses its appreciation of and desire for good, and, figuratively speaking, unhappy in God's presence and in the presence of righteous souls, says to evil, "Be thou my good," and asks for a bed among the swine. This is the unhappy state to which evil desires often bring their victims. How like these unclean spirits is the man who once had high purposes and noble ambitions, but now has become the victim of an evil desire—drink, or lust, or greed—and thinks only of the satisfying of that desire! He comes to a state in which his daily prayer is nothing else than "Send me into the swine."

[1] "Markheim."

There is a grim sequence in sin. One sin opens the way for another, suggests it, invites it, even demands it. In the days when tyrants did their will, one of those despots ordered a man into his presence and asked him what his calling was. When the man told him he was a blacksmith, the tyrant ordered him to go to his forge and make a chain. The man soon returned with a chain in his hand. "Go and make it longer," was the order of the tyrant. He soon appeared again, this time with a longer chain. "Go and make it still longer," was the order of the despot. This was repeated a number of times, and when finally the perplexed blacksmith appeared with a long chain in his hand, the despot ordered his soldiers to wrap the chain about the man and cast him into the fire. These were the wages for making the chain. So men by repeated indulgence are forging an ever lengthening chain with which they are to be bound and cast into the furnace of retribution and judgment.

Everywhere in life there are paths that lead upward and paths that lead downward; there are forces urging upward and those which have a downward pull. We have invitations to dwell with the angels and invitations to dwell with the swine, and man himself, armed with the mightiest of all weapons, his own will, must make the decision! Neither angels, men, nor demons can determine it for you. You must decide. There is no neutrality and no at-rest, stationary position in the moral world. There are just two directions—up or down—and just two goals.

Youth, above all the other periods of life, is the time when the two contrasting possibilities of life stand out. With its laughter and song and heedless mirth youth goes down the street in the springtime of life. But suppose we had the power to follow the destiny of each one of this army of youth. What history, what biography, we should then be able to write! Of some—and they are now as fair and full of promise as any in this happy and joyous procession of youth—the record will be that their souls became sensual, earthly, brutish, and that they entered into the swine; and of others, that they fought and struggled and prayed their way into the kingdom of God and into the company of the angels.

Perhaps you are saddened by the thought that, undeniably, the course of your recent life has been not upward and heavenward, but downward. If this is so, be of good courage. He who saved and healed the man on Gadara's hills can heal you and so change you that you will say, not "Send us into the swine," but "I will arise and go to my father."

XIII

"The mule that was under him
went away."

II Sam. 18:9

THE DOOM OF EVIL

"THE MULE THAT WAS UNDER HIM WENT AWAY." HE
always does! And there Absalom hangs, as he fled that
day from the field of battle, caught in the branches of the
tree by the luxurious tresses of that hair of which he was
so proud. There he hangs, all by himself, between heaven
and earth; deserted by his soldiers and even by his mule;
waiting there for the three fatal darts out of the hand of
Joab, and then for a last resting place in the pit in the
wood, with the stones of detestation and execration heaped
up over him. That was his grave and his monument. But
that was not the grave in which he had expected to lie;
for yonder in the king's dale he had built a costly
mausoleum which he proudly named after himself—
"Absalom's place." But no; it was not there that he was
buried, but in that pit in the wood.

When David's three divisions under the command of
Joab, Abishai, and Ittai marched out that morning to do
battle with Absalom and his rebel army in the wood of
Ephraim, David charged each commander as he went into
the battle, "Deal gently for my sake with the young man,
even with Absalom." He was fearful lest that brilliant

blackguard, his rebellious son, should perish in the battle, and his father's heart be broken.

And that was what happened. The untrained levies of Absalom were no match for the veteran troops of Joab, David's commander-in-chief, and were driven from the field with great slaughter. Absalom, riding on his royal mule, trying to escape the fate of his soldiers, rode into a detachment of David's army and, turning his mule about, galloped off in another direction. But as he passed through the forest, his head was caught in the boughs of a great oak, and his mule went from under him; and there he was left, hanging between heaven and earth. One of the soldiers saw him hanging there but refrained from laying a hand on him, for he remembered what David had said that morning, "Deal gently for my sake with the young man, even with Absalom." He reported the matter, however, to Joab, who rode up rapidly and, taking three darts from his hand, thrust them in quick succession through the heart of Absalom. Then ten young men of Joab's bodyguard drew their swords and buried them in the body of that rebellious prince.

During the battle David was waiting anxiously at the tower where his headquarters were established. The first runner, when asked by David, "Is the young man Absalom safe?" answered only, "I saw a great tumult, but I knew not what it was." He either did not know the fate of Absalom or was afraid to tell it to the king. But when the second runner appeared, and David asked him, "Is the young man Absalom safe?" he answered, "The enemies of my Lord the king, and all that rise against thee to do thee hurt, be as that young man is." David knew what that meant, and, wrapping his mantle about him, he went up the stone stairs to his chamber over the gate, and as he wept, he lamented: "O my son Absalom, my son, my son Absalom! would God I had died for thee, O Absalom, my son, my son!" That lament of brokenhearted David ended the history of Absalom.

EVIL BETRAYS THE EVILDOER

"The mule that was under went away." That mule preaches a memorable sermon, for he tells us that at length everything goes from under the evil man, the character that is not upright. What he rides on or trusts in fails him in the end. In the powerful language of the book of Job, "His confidence shall be rooted out . . . , and it shall bring him to the king of terrors." So Absalom was brought at length to the judgment, to the king of terrors.

There is always a fascination about ruins. We like to clamber over old moated castles and ruined forts. So in the Bible the shipwreck and ruin of great men always holds our interest: men like the eloquent Balaam, who had pronounced great blessings upon Israel and foretold its destiny, but who died in a wretched and sordid plot to corrupt the people whom he himself had not been able to curse, and so made them curse themselves; and Saul, the first king of Israel, who was head and shoulders over all Israel physically, and endued also with many splendid traits, but who, deserted by the prophet Samuel and by God, went to the cave of the witch of Endor, only to learn of his doom in the coming battle.

Absalom was not a great man, like some others in the Bible who made shipwreck in the end: like Gideon, who set up an idol even at Ophrah, where the angel of the

Lord had called him; or Solomon, the wisest and most glorious of kings, who in his old age was led astray by his wives and bowed his aged knees to false gods. Absalom was not a great man like these, but he was great, at least, in his talents and gifts. He was a man of imposing and beautiful presence. The record is that there was none so much praised for his beauty, and "from the sole of his foot even to the crown of his head there was no blemish in him." When he polled his golden hair at the end of the year, it weighed two hundred shekels. He had also an engaging personality and persuasive eloquence. In starting the rebellion against David he showed great skill and ability. He took his post by the gate, and when any citizen came to the king with a controversy and asked for judgment, Absalom would take him aside and ask him about his trouble, and when he had heard his story, he would exclaim, "Oh that I were made judge in the land, that every man which hath any suit or cause might come unto me, and I would do him justice!" So Absalom "stole the hearts of the men of Israel."

He had also high ambition, without which there can be no great life. He desired to hold a high place in the nation, and he wished his name to be remembered after his death. It was that which moved him to build for a tomb the costly pillar, Absalom's place, in the king's dale. In short, he seems to have been endued with every grace but the grace of God. And yet with all this, or in spite of all this, "the mule that was under him went away," and Absalom's once flawless and beautiful body was cast into the bottom of the pit in the wilderness, and stones were heaped over it. What was the secret of his ruin?

WHY ABSALOM FELL

One reason for the fall of Absalom was his selfishness. He is the supreme egoist of the Bible. He had high ambition, but it ended with himself. Immanuel Kant once said, "Treat every human being as a person, as an end in itself, not as a means to an end." But Absalom treated everybody as a means to his end. He admired no one. He had no sense of duty, no pity; and he did not scruple to mount, if he could, to the throne of Israel upon the corpse of his father. He whose ambition ends with himself will often find that his ambition ends him. That was true in the case of Absalom. The world will not stay long with the man whose only aim is self-glorification and self-exaltation. The highest ambition is not to rear a pillar, a grave that will be wondered at when you are dead, but to build an upright character with which to serve God and man. Jesus said, "whosoever exalteth himself shall be abased." No one illustrates that truth better than Absalom.

Another reason for Absalom's fall and ruin was irreverence. We sometimes speak of the three kinds of reverence—reverence for self, reverence for others, and reverence for God. Absalom had no reverence for himself. He did not hesitate to defile himself with treason and murder. John Randolph, that brilliant Virginian, used to say to young men, "Make to yourself an image, and in defiance of the Decalogue, worship it, whether it be excellence in medicine or law or political eminence." The advice is good, except for that one clause, "in defiance of the Decalogue." Absalom defied the Decalogue.

Another well-known character of the Old Testament who did not revere himself was Esau, whose epitaph in

140

the New Testament is "that profane person"—not profane in the sense of taking the name of God in vain, but profane in the sense of being unfenced, guarded by no principles and standards, "who for one morsel of meat sold his birthright." Absalom had a noble birthright. He was the son of a queen and the son of David; and when he was born, David named him Absalom, which means "the father of peace." But, alas, he was the father of woe and shame, both to himself and to others.

Again, Absalom had no reverence for others. He shunned not to slay his own brother, to defile his father's house, and to mount if possible to the throne of Israel on his father's dead body. In his rush for fame and power he trampled natural affection under his feet.

Absalom was totally lacking, too, in the third reverence —reverence for God. His dramatic story covers many pages in the Old Testament; and yet in nothing that Absalom says is there the slightest reference to God. He is the supreme illustration of the man whom the psalmist describes in the words, "God is not in all his thoughts." James G. Blaine, the brilliant statesman of the last quarter of the nineteenth century, in a letter to his son wrote, "There is no success in this life that is not founded on virtue and purity and religious consecration of all we have to God." And the wise man of the book of Proverbs said, "The fear of the Lord is the beginning of knowledge." And the apostle of the New Testament said, "Godliness is profitable unto all things, having promise of the life that now is, and of that which is to come." In the end the ungodly man loses out, both in this world and in the world to come. The mule goes from under him.

BRILLIANT BUT TRAGIC

The career of Absalom brings to mind two other brilliant men who were lacking in reverence for themselves, for others, and for God. One was Alcibiades, a famous Greek statesman and general. He was handsome in person, wealthy, dissipated, and a spendthrift. One day he served Athens; the next he was a traitor to Athens, conspiring with Sparta, the Syracusans, or the Persians. He used flattery, as Absalom did, and entered, or pretended to enter, into the interests and desires of other men. Plutarch in his famous *Lives* sagely remarks of Alcibiades that there was a saying or tradition that there was one color that the chameleon could not assume, and that color was white; but that Alcibiades, whether he was in the company of good men or bad men, adapted himself to his company and "wore equally the appearance of vice or virtue." In that respect he was like Absalom, and like Absalom he perished miserably at the hand of his enemies.

The other person whom the life of Absalom suggests was another very brilliant man, one of our own history, Aaron Burr. He had a noble ancestry and heritage. He was the grandson of Jonathan Edwards, whom Burr himself truly described as the "one clear thinker" America had produced. Burr had a quick and brilliant mind and made the highest record of his class in college. As an officer in the Army of the Revolution he was able and fearless. As a lawyer and as a statesman he was distinguished above his fellows. Yet as a man he failed, because he had no reverence for himself, for others, or for God. His political enemy, Alexander Hamilton, whom he afterward killed in a duel, wrote of him when Burr and Jefferson

142

were tied for the Presidency, "Every step in his career proves that he formed himself upon the model of Cataline." Thwarted and disappointed in his political ambitions, and heartbroken over the death of his beautiful and gifted daughter, Theodosia, Burr died at length in loneliness and poverty. At Princeton there is the tradition that during the Whitefield revivals he shut himself up in his room at college, vowing that he would settle the question of religion that night. Late that night students passing by saw the shutters of his window thrown open and heard him exclaim, "Good-by, God!"

Such, then, is the timeless teaching of the life of Absalom. "The mule that was under him went away." Always in the end—if not visibly here, then certainly in the judgment—the selfish, irreverent, godless life goes down. In one of the halls at West Point there are statues dedicated to distinguished officers of the armies of the United States. But there is one niche which is nameless. The name which ought to have been cut there is Benedict Arnold, who fought with such gallantry at Quebec and Saratoga, only to fall in the end and become a traitor to his country.

Look once more at those two monuments, those two graves of Absalom: first, the stately pillar in the king's dale, Absalom's place, built of marble and embellished with silver and gold, beautiful when the sun gilded its splendors at noonday and beautiful at night when the moon cast her ethereal mantle over it. But it is a tomb without a tenant. Then look at that other monument, the stone pile there in the wood of Ephraim, where Absalom, his body transfixed by the darts of Joab and hacked by the swords of Joab's bodyguard, lies buried like a dog, with only his brokenhearted father to weep over him.

XIV

"Then shalt thou break the bottle."

Jer. 19:10

LIFE'S IRREVOCABLE

IN THE GAUNT VALLEY OF HINNOM, TO THE SOUTHEAST of Jerusalem, a group of men are gathered together. One of them is speaking in tones of great earnestness, severity, and sadness. When he finishes his speech, he lifts his arm and, brandishing in the sunlight a finished potter's vessel, brings it crashing down on the rocks, where it is broken into fragments.

The speaker and actor is the prophet Jeremiah, who is prophesying at Jerusalem toward the sunset of the Hebrew monarchy, when the vultures of judgment and retribution are beginning to wheel over the doomed city. As to much of God's plan and purpose for it, the nation of Israel, through its obduracy and perversity and apostasy, had failed and come short. But even yet, through repentance and reformation, there could be a worth-while destiny. Even yet the vultures of retribution and judgment could be driven off.

To illustrate this truth Jeremiah is commanded to go down to the potter's house, still one of the most interesting places in the East. Of many of the great cities and civilizations of the past all that remains today is relics of the potter's craft. There is the potter seated on the ground, with the mass of clay near him, a vessel of water by his side, and in front of him the potter's wheel. When he has moistened and softened the clay, he puts it upon the horizontal wheel, and then, with the wheel revolving, with deft touch he begins to shape the vessel. When the vessel is near completion, he discovers that there is a serious flaw or dislocation in it. But because the clay is still soft and pliable, the potter is able to break down the vessel again and place the clay once more on the wheel, where he forms a new vessel, perhaps not just the same as the vessel that he had in mind when he started, but nevertheless something useful or ornamental. The meaning as applied to the nation is that although it has been seriously marred by disobedience and sin, and can never now be all that God had in mind for it, yet there is still possible for it a noble destiny.

But the second scene shows us something altogether different. It shows us the fate that Jerusalem is choosing for itself, one of utter rejection and judgment. This time Jeremiah is commanded to take a potter's vessel, one that has been finished and baked in the sun, or burned in the fire. It can never be changed now, like the other vessel which had been marred but was still soft and workable. Followed by the leaders of Israel, Jeremiah goes down into the grim valley of Hinnom. There he pronounces the coming judgment and doom upon Jerusalem. The land is to become desolate, and there will be a perpetual hissing, and the valley where they are standing will be covered with the slain. This is the doom that awaits the city because "they have hardened their necks, that they might not hear my words." At the conclusion of these words of judgment and of doom Jeremiah breaks the potter's bottle to fragment on the rocks. "Even so will I break this people and this city, as one breaketh a potter's vessel, that cannot be made whole again."

These parables acted by Jeremiah expressed a truth which applies primarily to the nations; but since nations are made up of individuals, we have here a striking and timeless expression of important truth. First, that God has a plan for every life and that every life has a great possibility. Second, that failures and mistakes and sins need not be final and fatal. And third, that there comes a time when character is fixed and destiny is chosen and determined. No change can then be made.

THE GREAT POSSIBILITIES OF EVERY LIFE

When God created man in his image—the creation that has been repeated with the coming of every new life into the world—he spoke the great truth that every life has high possibilities and that God has a plan for every life. Out of the native clay of man's nature what wonderful things can be coined! On a visit to Tuskegee Institute I saw in the museum some of the paintings of the Negro scientist and artist Dr. Carver. There were exquisite reds and greens and blues and purples which he had produced out of ordinary clay, just ordinary Alabama clay.

If you give a potter at the potter's house a lump of clay, there is no telling what he will be able to get out of that sordid clay. Ages ago an unknown potter or sculptor in Greece decided to make something beautiful. He put the clay on his wheel and fashioned it into an urn, and on the urn he put youths and maidens, gods and goddesses, forests and streams, a mountain citadel, and a little town down by the sea. The urn was sold to some wealthy Greek to adorn his home by the sea. The potter or sculptor who made the urn passed away. The wealthy man who bought the urn passed away. The age in which it was bought, and age after age in succession, passed away. But in some way that urn survived the vicissitudes of the centuries and found its way across the seas to the British Museum. There one day a livery stable helper, with the fire of consumption in his veins, but with the fire of genius in his heart and in his eyes, looked upon the urn that the ancient sculptor of Greece had made; and as he looked, he wrote the lines of his famous ode which will last as long as the English language:

> Thou still unravished bride of quietness,
>   Thou foster-child of Silence and slow Time,
> Sylvan historian, who canst thus express
>   A flowery tale more sweetly than our rhyme. . .[1]

Just ordinary Greek clay, and yet out of it a beautiful urn, and John Keats's immortal ode. So out of the clay of life, if men yield themselves to the Potter's hand and to the Potter's plan, things of beauty and of usefulness can be made. But how many marred and broken vessels there are, useless and unattractive, that might have been a blessing to mankind.

That word that God spoke to Abraham he speaks to every life when he calls it to serve him, "Thou shalt be a blessing." The word that Samuel spoke to the amazed Saul when he anointed him king over Israel is a prophetic word for every life, "On whom is all the desire of Israel? Is it not on thee?" So many millions of lives come into the world and leave the world, and yet for every one the

---

[1] "Ode on a Grecian Urn."

Great Designer has a plan and a purpose. Yield yourself to his hand, yield yourself to his plan, and you will know how

> There's a divinity that shapes our ends,
> Rough-hew them how we will.

MARRED BOTTLES AND MARRED LIVES CAN BE MENDED

Here we come to deal with another great and beautiful truth of life, the restorations of life. All sin mars and defiles, and yet by the grace of God these sins and mistakes can be overcome. This truth is brought out by the first of the two scenes described in this passage from the book of Jeremiah. At the potter's house we saw the potter take a vessel which had been marred but which, because its substance was still soft and formative, could be recast and remolded into another vessel.

In how many different ways men mar their souls! By the waste of time, instead of redeeming the time; by the failure to respond immediately to the gracious impulses and invitations of the Holy Spirit; by compromise with evil; and by positive sin. It is therefore a blessed thing that the plan of God for our lives includes the possibility of restoration. "Cannot I do with you as this potter? saith the Lord." God claims it as his right to remake us and to remold us, and the gospel of Christ is the declaration that it is his desire and his love to do so.

This is one of the most inspiring things about human life, that God gives men a second chance and opportunity, and that a vessel that has been marred or disfigured, by repentance and new obedience can be remolded and refashioned into something of use and beauty. Jacob was a marred vessel. He was the son of great promise and of high election. But what a sordid, lying, deceiving, cowardly man he was; until one night he wrestled with the angel of God, who changed him from Jacob, the supplanter and deceiver, to Israel, the man who had power with God. Manasseh, the old King of Judah who did more wickedness in his long reign than any who went before him or came after him, was a marred vessel; and yet in his old age and in his captivity he turned again to the God of his father, Hezekiah, and God restored him to his kingdom; and the remainder of Manasseh's reign was as illustrious for piety and good works as the former part had been for wickedness and apostasy.

David was a marred vessel. How wonderful and beautiful a vessel God had in mind when he created David! How gifted and noble a life. But alas! David marred his vessel—marred it with his triple transgression of adultery, murder, and hypocrisy. But God still had use for David. David repented. He prayed, "Cast me not away from thy presence; and take not thy holy spirit from me. Restore unto me the joy of thy salvation. . . . Then will I teach transgressors thy ways." David asked for another chance, and God gave it to him. Not only was he forgiven, but he was restored; and today David preaches from every pulpit, sings from every hymnbook and psalm book; his Twenty-third Psalm is the pillow of comfort under the head of the sufferer in the hospital, and the companion upon which the soul leans as it goes down into the cold waters of the river of death.

Peter was a marred vessel. His original call, the honors and distinctions and the special instruction that Christ gave him, he repaid with an enormous transgression. Yet when he repented and was converted, God called him back to feed his flock and to become the great leader of his church, a rock now no longer in name only, but in fact and in character.

John Mark was a marred vessel. When he turned back at Perga, on the Gulf of Antalya, where Paul and Barnabas began their ascent through the wild mountain country in the direction of Antioch of Pisidia, it looked as if complete failure and disgrace were to cover his name. On the next journey, when they were ready to leave Antioch, Paul refused to permit Mark to go with them. He would have nothing to do with such a man. But from the subsequent history we know that Mark had another chance, and that he repented of his cowardice and weakness, and showed himself useful and faithful as a Christian disciple and helper of the apostles; for in one of the last messages that we have from Paul he asks Timothy to come to him in the prison at Rome, and to bring Mark with him, "for he is profitable to me for the ministry."

Augustine was a marred vessel. He was a youth of careful training and noble inheritance, and had one of the great mothers of history, the devout and gifted Monica. Yet we learn from Augustine's *Confessions* that as early as the age of sixteen he plunged into the cesspool of sexual impurity, an abyss in which he continued to wallow until the day of his conversion, sixteen years later in the garden at Milan. Repeatedly called by this providence, by that danger or affliction, or by the appeals of his beloved mother, Augustine tried to deliver himself out of this filthy bondage of the flesh, only to fall back into sin. At length at Milan he came under the teaching of Ambrose, and the Spirit of God began to work in his heart. One memorable morning in the garden as he wept and prayed, he heard a voice saying, "Take and read, take and read." Then, taking up the letters of Paul, his eye fell on this passage, "Put ye on the Lord Jesus Christ and make no provision for the flesh, to fulfill the lust thereof." The reading of that passage brought the long struggle to a conclusion, and Augustine knelt at the foot of the Cross a penitent and a follower of Jesus Christ, and one who henceforth was to do great things for Christ and for his kingdom.

This truth of the possibility of divine restoration and of how the marred vessel of life can be remade is one that has a particular meaning for those of us who are in the Church of Christ. We have all come short of what we might have been, and what we have no doubt desired to be as a confessed follower of Christ and as a member of his Church. Some of you have neglected the means of grace: the Bible and prayer and worship. Others have thrown the whole strength and enthusiasm of your lives into the things of this world and left very little for the Church. Others have fallen into habits that have marred your Christian lives, or you have formed companionships and associations which do not honor your profession and do not honor Christ. But, thank God, if you will have him do it, if even now you will repent and turn to him, he can remake your marred vessel and mold you into a vessel meet for the Master's use.

In an eloquent speech delivered at the centennial celebration of Jefferson College, now Washington and Jefferson, one of the orators referred to the well-known fact that Michelangelo's stirring sculpture at Florence of David slaying Goliath, the replica of which stands on a hill overlooking the city, was fashioned out of a block of marble which another artist had been working on and which, when he had marred it, he had cast aside as useless. The speaker then went on to say that in some remote part of the world there might be an old alumnus of the college who had not made of himself what he might have made; had not fulfilled the promise of his college days and the hopes of his family and his friends; had betrayed his soul and marred the vessel of his life through sin. If so, on this day, the old college flung out her voice to her wayward son inviting him to return to honor and to God. Even yet, although the original pattern was not possible, something worthy and useful and honorable could be made out of his life.

THE IRREVOCABLE AND THE UNCHANGEABLE IN LIFE

God has a plan for every man. There is a high possibility for every life, and yet we cannot pass over the other truth that is taught here, and that is that there is also an irrevocable and unchangeable in life. This truth is brought out in the second scene, in which Jeremiah breaks the potter's vessel, completely finished, hardened in the sun and burned in the fire. The vessel now cannot be changed or worked over; neither when it is broken can it be made whole again.

The bottle was broken into fragments. Here we have the warning and the solemnity of the irrevocable. How often we hear the echo of the crash of that broken bottle! I have heard it in the calamities and tragedies which have overtaken men and women in the way of sin, who have found that the way of the transgressor is hard. A month ago, six months ago, a year ago, they might have turned back, and judgment might have been averted; but they refused to be wise, and they spurned the warning of conscience and the appeal of God's Holy Spirit. Now they realize with sadness and bitterness what has been lost and can never be found and restored again.

I have heard the crash of that broken bottle of opportunity and possibility in the chamber of the dead and in the cemetery, so littered with the glass of broken bottles of last chance. There I have heard its echo in the sad sentences or stifled sobs of those who realize that something they once might have done, and always ought to have done, is now forever impossible. They would give all that they possess if now they could speak to the dead what they failed to speak, or take back the words they spoke, or do the thing they left undone, or undo what they have done; but all alike is impossible now. O Death, arrest for a moment thy lifted arm! Stay for a moment thy inexorable sentence, and break not yet the bottle of my chance and opportunity! But death is inexorable. The soul now faces the irrevocable. Crash! and the bottle is broken upon the headstone of the tomb.

I have heard the echo of that broken bottle in the lament of the holy angels, the guardian spirits, over the finally impenitent. The day once was when in spite of past mistakes and past rejections of the Holy Spirit they might have believed and been saved. Once they might have heard the music of the angels' song of welcome. Once they might have heard the music of the Savior's "Well done, . . . enter thou into the joy of thy Lord." But instead of that, what they hear now is the lament of the holy angels and the sorrowful words of Christ, "If thou hadst known . . . the things which belong unto thy peace! but

153

now they are hid from thine eyes, . . . because thou knewest not the time of thy visitation."

The time of thy visitation! How precious, beautiful, and memorable is that day! And, thank God, for every one of us today this is still the day of opportunity and of visitation. Still, regardless of what the past may have held, whatever failure, neglect, transgression, sin, or grieving of the Holy Ghost, still the precious vessel of life can be changed and remolded and refashioned by repentance and by faith. And in a moment of time that can be done! In a moment of time what long years have written can be erased. In a moment of time what the years have marred can be changed. Oh, how wonderful and gracious is our God! "O the depth of the riches both of the wisdom and knowledge of God! how unsearchable are his judgments, and his ways past finding out!" "Seek ye the Lord while he may be found, call ye upon him while he is near." While he is near!

XV

> "I will give thee two thousand horses,
> if thou be able on thy part to set
> riders upon them." Isa. 36:8

HORSES TO THOSE WHO CAN RIDE

THIS IS A LEAF TORN FROM THE ANCIENT HISTORY OF Jerusalem, when Sennacherib besieged the city and "the Assyrian came down like the wolf on the fold." Held up by the siege of the stronghold of Lachish, Sennacherib sent one of his generals, Rabshakeh, on to Jerusalem to demand the surrender of the city. The speech of Rabshakeh was a curious combination of bombast, blasphemy, and boasting. He even went the length of claiming that Sennacherib's invasion of Judah was undertaken by divine authority, and that Hezekiah himself, who had destroyed the high places in Judah, was the enemy of God. He warned the people of Jerusalem against reliance upon deliverance from their trouble by the help of Egypt. It would be folly for them to let Hezekiah persuade them that the Lord would deliver them. It would fare with them just as it had fared with other cities which had put their confidence in their gods and had consequently been taken and sacked by Sennacherib. Rabshakeh called the roll of those cities and bade the besieged Jews look at the trail of smoke and ashes which Sennacherib's army had left behind it.

The insulting speech of Rabshakeh reached its climax

when he taunted the ambassadors of Hezekiah with the military impotence of Jerusalem. How could they resist Sennacherib when they had no army with which to oppose him? Even if he, Rabshakeh, were to loan them two thousand cavalry horses, it would do them no good, for they had no soldiers to mount them. They could not stand against even a single captain of a small detachment of Sennacherib's army, not to speak of resisting the whole host of Assyria. As events turned out, Sennacherib learned that Jerusalem and the people of God had defenses and resources other than soldiers and horses and chariots of war. God stretched forth his hand and smote the camp of the Assyrians. "The angel of the Lord went out, and smote in the camp of the Assyrians an hundred fourscore and five thousand: and when they arose early in the morning, behold, they were all dead corpses."

> For the Angel of Death spread his wings on the blast,
> And breathed in the face of the foe as he passed;
> And the eyes of the sleepers waxed deadly and chill,
> And their hearts but once heaved, and for ever grew
> still! [1]

LIFE AND OPPORTUNITY

Taken by itself, as a part of the record of the siege of Jerusalem, Rabshakeh's speech is just a masterpiece of biting and insulting sarcasm. But lifted out of the context, his words are a striking statement of an important and ever timely truth: namely, that opportunity and power and influence are offered to men in this life, but only to those who are qualified to make use of them.

[1] Byron, "The Destruction of Sennacherib."

Rabshakeh said he would offer two thousand horses to the beleaguered citizens of Jerusalem; but it would do them no good, because they had no soldiers to ride these horses. Thus this braggart, this blatant and blasphemous satrap, Rabshakeh, becomes an eloquent preacher, and his theme is the chance and opportunity which life gives to us and the way men use or lose their opportunity.

Horses to those who can ride! Talents to those who can make use of them. Increased powers to those who have proved their worth. If a college education is of the great advantage which it is claimed to be, then there never was so fortunate an age as our own, for education has become almost universal. Whether you estimate it by theory or by experiment, an education gives one a great start and advantage in the race of life. The educated man is given a horse to ride, while the multitude must go on foot. But this advantage does not make the man or insure success in life. Horses are no use to you if you are not able to mount and ride them.

When I was in college, the country was stirred by the excitement of the events in Cuba, culminating in the blowing up of the battleship *Maine* in the Havana harbor, and the war with Spain. The leader of the Spanish rebels was General Garcia. Our government wished to send a secret communication to him. An officer by the name of Rowan was chosen. He landed in Cuba and managed to make his way through the Spanish lines into the camp of the insurrectionists, where he delivered the message to Garcia. The next year Elbert Hubbard published his famous story, "The Message to Garcia," telling of the exploits of Rowan. This story attained an extraordinary circulation of forty million and made Hubbard famous. Business executives and employers all over the world eagerly seized upon it and put it into circulation. The reason was that in "The Message to Garcia" Hubbard, instead of presenting the familiar and overdone idea that men of ability and of willing mind are on the search for a place and for work they can do, developed the other idea: namely, that places of importance are waiting for the man who can fill them, and that the world is calling for men like Rowan, who can get the message through to Garcia. It was a good idea, and an ever timely one.

This is a truth that is frequently enforced and illustrated in the Scriptures. Perhaps the best illustration of it—the fact that after all opportunities and advantages are given a man, their worth depends upon his own character—is found in our Lord's parable of the talents. Although the three men received different sums, one ten talents, the other five, and the third one, all of them by reason of that special gift had something beyond others, an unusual opportunity. Two of them succeeded, but the third failed miserably, and the reason of his failure was not lack of opportunity or lack of ability or other advantage, but lack of character. That was why he failed. When the day of reckoning came, those who proved themselves able by their character to use the opportunity which was presented unto them were rewarded with larger gifts and new opportunities; whereas the man who had done nothing and who had failed through lack of character lost all that he had. "Whosoever hath, to him shall be given, . . . but whosoever hath not, from him shall be taken even that he hath."

Without character there can be no true success, and the lack of character disqualifies men from making use of the powers and opportunities which life has presented to them. Lincoln's great secretary of war, Edwin M. Stanton, refused to let his son attend some night classes in chemistry to which he had been invited, on the ground that by going out at night at his tender age he might fall in with bad company. The boy's morals were paramount to all the education he could get, the father said.

When the great Senator LaFollette, father of the two sons of more recent years, was first elected governor of Wisconsin, his old friend John Bascom, the noted philosopher of Williams College who had been president of Wisconsin when LaFollette was a student there, wrote to him: "Robert, you will doubtless make mistakes of judgment as governor. But never mind the political mistakes, as long as you make no ethical mistakes." Likewise Judge Bryan, the father of William Jennings Bryan, said to his son when he went out into the world: "You can afford to be defeated, but you can never afford to be wrong."

The lack of industry will disqualify a man from mounting the horse of usefulness and influence which has been brought to his gate. Winston Churchill, the well-known British statesman, did not have the advantage of a university education but was trained in a military school. He regretted in after life that he did not have the great advantage of a training at Oxford or Cambridge. In his book *My Early Life, A Roving Commission* he gives expression to that regret; but then he adds: "But I now pity undergraduates, when I see what frivolous lives many of them lead in the midst of precious, fleeting opportunity. After all, a man's life must be nailed to a cross, either of thought or of action. Without work, there is no play."

Life is so generous and freehanded in what it offers to us; but when we neglect or scorn her offer, then life is inexorable.

TEMPTATION AND OPPORTUNITY

Where opportunity is the more abundant, there temptation is the more seductive and powerful. Last year I visited the preparatory school in California which I attended years ago. Then it was a small struggling school with plain living and high thinking. Today it is greatly increased in this world's goods, and as is the rule where riches have increased, religion and Christian ideals have declined. Where once I walked between the cactus and the sage brush, there is now a stately avenue, and at the entrance to the campus there is a beautiful stone arch. On the outside of the arch and greeting every student as he enters the campus for the first time these words are cut: "Let only the earnest, thoughtful, and reverent enter here." Perhaps the time will come when less attention will be paid to the scholarly qualifications of a graduate, and more to the qualifications of character for entrance and matriculation. In the school of life reverence for the high and holy things of life is a condition of true success.

Once there was a young king who ruled over a vast kingdom, Babylon. No young man ever held a greater opportunity. But he lost his kingdom in a single night, a single night of revelry and drunkenness. It is recorded of him that he went so far in his drunken folly as to drink wine out of the sacred vessels of the temple which had been brought from Jerusalem. His sacrilegious folly was his fall, for "in that night was Belshazzar the king of the Chaldeans slain." His end tells the story of what lack of reverence will do to a man's life, and how it will strip him of his crown. Horses to those who can ride them, and crowns to those who are fit to wear them.

The temptations of the flesh, if yielded to, disqualify a man from riding the horse of influence and of usefulness. Recently I met a man who belonged to a family which I had known in my boyhood days. We spoke of his father and a brother who had died, of the old homestead and incidents of former days. But there was one member of the family whom he did not mention, nor did I inquire concerning him, although of all the family it was he who stood out most vividly in my memory. Highly gifted, so far as talent and ability were concerned, fitted and qualified to ride in the front ranks of the world's crusaders, the man failed dismally through lack of character. His shield was vilely cast away, as if he had not been anointed with oil.

Those who would control others must first learn to control themselves. Self-knowledge, self-reverence, self-control, these three alone lead life to sovereign power.

Alexander the Great was great also as a horseman. One day, as a youth, he saw the beautiful black horse Bucephalus about to be rejected by the king's officers because he plunged and reared and kicked when anyone tried to mount him. Alexander begged Philip to let him ride this horse. He had noted that the horse was frightened by his shadow. After the holding straps had been removed, he turned the head of Bucephalus toward the sun, spoke reassuringly to him, vaulted gracefully to his back, and then, in full control of the horse, cantered about the field, to the admiration of Philip and all who were present. Alexander knew how to ride and to control himself, as well as a horse. In one of his campaigns in India he was desperately wounded by an arrow. He was laid on a table, and his comrades were about to cut the shaft from his side. As was the custom, since they had no mystic anesthetic to dull the edge of pain, they laid hold of his arms to hold him while the painful operation was performed. But Alexander waved them aside, saying as he did so, "There is no need to hold him who is able to hold himself."

We hear a great deal today about the new age and the new thought and the new conditions and all that; but it is just as well to remember that there is no such thing as a new man. Man is just what he was when the Bible was written and when Christ died for him. The Ten Commandments still strike inexorably at the man who violates them, and the broken moral law smites just as hard as ever the man who breaks it.

Hartley Coleridge, son of the great poet and himself a man of great gifts and capacity, once went back to Oxford, where amid beautiful surroundings and wonderful opportunities he had spent his days in dissipation and folly. Looking on the ancient ivy-covered buildings and the lovely grounds, he exclaimed aloud, "To think that in such a place I lived such a life!" Nothing could be sadder than the situation of a man who has the ability and the knowledge and the desire to act or strike or speak in behalf of right and truth, some holy cause of God or man, but who, just when he would speak or act or strike, feels upon his arm the arresting and paralyzing touch of some folly and sin of the past, which says to him, "This is not your battle. You belong to me."

FAITH SUPREME

Faith is the greatest weapon for the battle of life. Sometimes the college student permits the facts of the temporal, the visible, world to eclipse the facts of the moral world. But the greatest facts are not the facts of star dust or protoplasm, but the facts of the soul, of salvation, of destiny. Here is a youth who has entered the armory of life to be panoplied for the battle. He sees the sword of knowledge and says, "Give me that sword! I can use it." And then the sword of wit: "That is a useful sword; let me have it!" And then the sword of eloquence: "Give me that sword. I can fight well with it." And then the sword of personality and charm: "Let me have that sword, too." But when he is offered the sword of faith, he says, "No; I do not need that sword. It was all right for my father and grandfather; but now it is an outmoded and discarded weapon." But the youth who thus speaks and thinks makes a profound mistake, for the sword of faith flashes and smites when all other swords have snapped and have been trampled in the dust of the arena.

When King Arthur was dying after his last battle, he gave his famous sword, Excalibur, to Sir Bedivere, and charged him to hurl it into the sea. When he did so, an arm, white and mystic, rose out of the sea, brandished the sword aloft three times, and drew it under. A true parable of life! He fights longest and most victoriously who fights with the sword which comes out of the invisible, the sword of faith.

Paul charged Timothy to remember Jesus Christ. That is always the safe, the wise, the stirring, and the heroic thing to do: Remember Jesus Christ! Take him as your example, your friend and companion, and by his death on the cross your Saviour; and the gate is open for you to the best there is in life. Reading his Bible one night, Thomas Carlyle paused and, looking up, exclaimed, "Jesus Christ! Higher than that, human thought cannot go!"

XVI

"Wherefore did Sarah laugh?"

Gen. 18:13

THE LAUGHTER OF EARTH AND HEAVEN

WHY DID SARAH LAUGH? LAUGHTER IS ONE OF GOD'S greatest gifts to man. At least two great gifts of God to man have survived the wreck and ruin of the fall: laughter, which for the moment, at least, causes man to forget his sorrow and his care; and beautiful, incomparable, invincible hope, which paints with the iridescent colors of the rainbow the horizon of man's ofttimes stormy and clouded life. We all like to hear a man laugh, and we all enjoy a good laugh ourselves. As the wise man said in the book of Proverbs, "A merry heart doeth good like a medicine."

There are many kinds of laughter. There is the innocent laughter at the ridiculous and absurd, the scornful laughter, a secret laughter as when one "laughs up his sleeve"; the laughter of delirium, the laughter of the maniac, the laughter at the obscene and vile. Whether laughter is good for the soul or not depends upon the kind of laughter. The Bible describes at least four different kinds of laughter: the laughter of incredulity and unbelief, the laughter of the fool, God's laughter, and the laughter of heaven.

THE LAUGHTER OF INCREDULITY
AND UNBELIEF

It was the early afternoon, and at the encampment of Abraham at Hebron, as was—and still is—the custom in those countries, all life was at a standstill. Ishmael, the child of Hagar, was asleep. The sheep and the goats were huddled together under the oaks at Mamre. Abraham was sitting in the shadows before his black tent. Suddenly, although he had been looking along the road that led to Hebron from the north and had seen no travelers, he was aware of the presence of three men. There was something very mysterious about the presence of those three men. Christian thought and worship have often seen in their visit to the tent of Abraham an early manifestation of the doctrine of the Holy Trinity. There were three who appeared, and yet it was One, the Lord, or Jehovah, who spoke; and it was One, the Lord, to whom Abraham spoke. The doctrine of the Trinity—that there are three persons in the Godhead, that the Father is God, that the Son is God, and that the Holy Spirit is God—is the foundation of our Christian faith. And yet it is sublime mystery before which we bow in adoration, crying, "Holy, holy, holy, Lord God of Hosts!"

After Abraham had greeted his visitors with true oriental courtesy, the One who was the Lord, or Jehovah, told Abraham that his wife, Sarah, would bear a child. This was a promise which had been made to Abraham long ago. When he came up out of Mesopotamia and Ur of the Chaldees, God told him that a great nation would spring from his loins. But after years had passed and there was no sign of a child and heir through whom the promise would be fulfilled, Abraham spoke to God with something of a note of discouragement, and was bold enough, and reverent enough, too, to remind God that he had given him no child. When he said this, the Lord spoke to him and said, as they looked up into the brilliant eastern sky strewn with multitudinous stars like golden dust, "Look now toward heaven, and tell the stars, if thou be able to number them: and he said unto him, So shall thy seed be." And Abraham "believed in the Lord; and he counted it to him for righteousness."

But again years passed by, and there was no child. Sarah herself had given up hope, and Abraham acquiesced in her suggestion that perhaps God might fulfill the promise through a child by the bondwoman, Hagar. But that was not God's way; and the plan which they followed brought only sorrow and bitterness to Sarah, to Hagar, to Abraham, and to Hagar's son.

Once more the promise was renewed by this mysterious One who visited Abraham at the oaks of Mamre. He told Abraham that Sarah should bear a child. Sarah, who was listening behind the tent to the conversation, laughed. And one might say, "No wonder!" Abraham was ninety-nine years of age, and Sarah was not far behind. "Impossible! Unthinkable! Contrary to all nature and experience," Sarah thought to herself. She did not laugh audibly, and her laugh was not heard by Abraham or anyone else save the Lord, for Sarah "laughed within herself." Yet the Lord heard it. God knows all your inmost thoughts. When you laugh or cry or doubt or scoff within yourself, God knows it. From him no secret is hidden. He tries the reins and searches our thoughts.

The Lord said to Abraham, "Why did Sarah laugh?" Then God said what has become one of the greatest statements of the Bible—"Is any thing too hard for the Lord?" Sarah, frightened, appeared and sought to defend herself by denying that she had laughed. But God said, "Thou didst laugh." In the course of time the great promise was fulfilled. Sarah gave birth to a child and called his name Isaac, saying, "God hath made me to laugh." But this time it was not the laugh of incredulity and unbelief, but the laughter of unexpected joy.

Reading this story, one will think of a promise that was given concerning the birth of a child to another woman, not a nonagenarian like Sarah, but an unmarried virgin. When the angel told Mary that she would bear a child, she, too, was puzzled and perplexed, and she said, "How shall this be?" But Gabriel said to her, "With God nothing shall be impossible," just as the Lord had said to Sarah, "Is anything too hard for the Lord?" The difference between Mary and Sarah was that Mary bowed herself in humble faith and belief, whereas Sarah laughed in unbelief.

Sarah's laugh was the laugh of incredulity and doubt. It has had a long echo in the world. Our Christian faith presents to us propositions and promises which to the natural mind, and judged by human experience and standards, are as incredible as that Sarah in her great age should bear a child. It asks us to believe that this world, so often wet with blood and wet with tears and darkened with war and hate and injustice, is nevertheless under the rule and government of a God who is infinitely powerful and wise and good, who does his will in the armies of heaven and among the inhabitants of the earth; and that "the end of the Lord" will be the triumph of justice and righteousness.

Students at Princeton at the turn of the century, in the university and in the theological seminary, will remember how President Francis L. Patton was wont to quote in his sermons the words:

> O, yet we trust that somehow good
> Will be the final goal of ill,
> To pangs of nature, sins of will,
> Defects of doubt, and taints of blood;
>
> That nothing walks with aimless feet;
> That not one life shall be destroy'd,
> Or cast as rubbish to the void,
> When God hath made the pile complete.[1]

But it takes real trust and faith to believe that. Again, our Christian faith asks us to believe that God intervened in the history of this planet by sending his only begotten Son to redeem the world by his atoning death on the cross; and that one day he will draw all men unto him; and also that one day he will intervene again in the history of this planet when Christ shall come in glory. Furthermore, our Christian faith tells us as we look upon the beloved dead and wonder at the pulseless hand, the silent lips, the rayless eye, that this is not the end of man's chapter; that this corruptible must put on incorruption, that this mortal must put on immortality; and that then

[1] Tennyson, "In Memoriam."

death, now so universal, so merciless, so seemingly un-conquerable, shall be "swallowed up in victory."

All this requires faith. Yet in this world we walk, we march, by faith. "By faith Abel," "by faith Noah," "by faith Abraham," "by faith Moses," "by faith Paul;" and by the same faith you and I. Courage is not a rare virtue. Sympathy, pity, is not a rare virtue. Abhorrence of evil is not rare. But great faith is rare. How often Christ must say to you and me what he said to those frightened dis-ciples after he had stilled the tempest that stormy night on Gennesaret, "Where is your faith?" When God puts you to the test, remember what he said to Sarah, "Is anything too hard for the Lord?"

THE LAUGHTER OF THE FOOL

The book of Ecclesiastes has a good deal to say on that subject. Among other things, "As the crackling of thorns under a pot, so is the laughter of the fool."

An annual event—and for the children a great and stirring one—in our home was when the hillside between the house and the river was burned over every spring. I can remember how the fallen branches, the dead leaves, and the heaped-up thorns burned brightly and fiercely for a little while, and then went out as quickly as they had burned. So is the laughter of the fool. It has no content, no abiding meaning, to it.

In the Bible the fool seems to describe the man who is foolish enough to set himself against God, or even deny that there is a God. "The fool hath said in his heart [not in his mind], There is no God." I suppose it was that kind of scoffing and laughter that Robert Burns had in mind when he wrote:

> The great Creator to revere
> Must sure become the creature;
>
> .   .   .   .   .   .
>
> An atheist-laugh's a poor exchange
> For Deity offended! [2]

But we take now the laughter of the fool in a wider sense—that is, foolish laughter. A sum that would stagger our imagination, should we try to calculate it, is invested today in the radio, the newspaper comics, television, and movies for the purpose of making people laugh. I suppose never before in the history of mankind have so many thousands of people laughed at the same time. Much of this laughter, no doubt, is wholesome. And yet we sometimes wonder how many of the thousands upon thousands who join in this nightly chorus of laughter—some of it wholesome, some of it unwholesome—have other thoughts of the seriousness and earnestness of life. Some of them do; and no doubt some of them realize that, after all, what they have laughed at has nothing which abides, nothing which can feed the soul. It is like the crackling of thorns under the pot, the fire which springs up quickly and as quickly goes out. The book of Psalms, which strikes every chord in that marvelous harp which God hath strung in every heart, opens with a grand statement about the happiness which abides, for "blessed" is the Old Testament word for "happy." "Blessed is the man that walketh not in the counsel of the ungodly, . . . but his delight is in the law of the Lord. . . . He shall be like a tree planted by the rivers of water, that bringeth forth his fruit in his season."

[2] "Epistle to a Young Friend."

GOD'S LAUGHTER

The Second Psalm describes the revolt of the natural mind and the natural man against God. "Why do the heathen rage, and the people imagine a vain thing? The kings of the earth set themselves, and the rulers take counsel together, against the Lord, and against his anointed, saying, Let us break their bands asunder, and cast away their cords from us."

This great psalm was written centuries ago. But it is still up-to-date and is a true description of the world today. There is, first of all, in the Communistic propaganda and philosophy an open revolt against God. Godlessness seems to be the very heart of this doctrine, and that accounts, in part, for Communism's present sway over the minds of men. But elsewhere, and in countries not on the other side of the Iron Curtain, but on this side, there is a revolt against God. These cords and bands of moral sanctions and prohibitions and commandments are to be broken asunder; these cords of restraint are to be cast from us. Much of the education, much of the science, much of the politics, much of the social philosophy, is frankly anti-God.

But now in this great psalm the scene changes from earth to heaven, from man's conspiracy and revolt to God's judgment and the overthrow of the wicked. "He that sitteth in the heavens shall laugh: the Lord shall have them in derision. Then shall he speak unto them in his wrath, and vex them in his sore displeasure." That has been the ultimate history of all revolts against God. They tried it in the French Revolution; they abolished the Christian Sabbath, established a week of eight days,

172

and worshiped the goddess of reason. But in the heavens God laughed, and men laugh today at their folly.

When those who had conspired with Adolf Hitler were asked by the judge, after their conviction in the Nuremburg trials, if they had anything to say, some were silent, others scoffed and were defiant, and others boasted of their deeds. But one who had held a high post gave a different testimony. He said: "The way of Hitler was the way of unbelief in Christ; and therefore the way of ruin, of judgment, and of death."

I am glad that the Bible tells us God laughed. When I am troubled by what I see going on in the world, kings and princes of thought taking counsel against God, and the cardinal doctrines of our holy faith flouted and denied even within the church itself, I like to look up and listen for God's laughter. Yet God, who laughs and judges and overthrows the wicked, nevertheless loves them; and, as in this psalm, he appeals to them and beseeches them to be wise and instructed; to kiss the Son, to be reconciled unto God in Christ. That is ever the message of the gospel, and without it there is no true gospel. As the Apostle said, "We pray you in Christ's stead, be ye reconciled to God."

THE LAUGHTER OF HEAVEN

We know that there will be laughter in heaven, for Jesus said in Luke's variant of the Sermon on the Mount, "Blessed are ye that weep now: for ye shall laugh." When the exiles in Babylon came back to Jerusalem, this is what they said and what they sang: "When the Lord turned again the captivity of Zion, we were like them that dream. Then was our mouth filled with laughter, and our tongue with singing: then said they among the heathen, The Lord hath done great things for them. The Lord hath done great things for us; whereof we are glad."

But that was not the way they had felt a short time before. Then, in the land of their captivity, Jerusalem, in ruins and desolation, had seemed so far off from Babylon, and the power of Babylon, the power of them that had carried them away captive, had seemed so great and irresistible that, although Jerusalem came often and tenderly into their minds, they could not believe that they would ever see the city of David again. No; what they felt was this: "By the rivers of Babylon, there we sat down, yea, we wept, when we remembered Zion. We hanged our harps upon the willows in the midst thereof. For there they that carried us away captive required of us a song; and they that wasted us required of us mirth, saying, Sing us one of the songs of Zion. How shall we sing the Lord's song in a strange land?"

That was the way they felt. But once again it was proved that nothing is "too hard for the Lord," and that "with God nothing shall be impossible." Although Cyrus knew him not, God girded him and made him his shepherd and the agent of his will; and the Lord "turned again the captivity of Zion."

What a day it was for those returning captives when first they looked again on the walls of Zion! Today, when even the most careless and formal Christian sees for the first time the walls of Jerusalem, he must feel, to a degree at least, a stirring and uplifting of his soul. Today—and I have seen some of them on their journey—the Jew who returns from afar to the land of Judah and

David's city must feel within his heart what can be felt only by a Jew, by one who has often said to himself what the Lord said to his people, "Let Jerusalem come into your mind." If that is true of a Christian visitor to Jerusalem today, and of a Jew returning to Israel today, then what shall we say of those Hebrew captives who not long before had hanged their harps on the willows and sat down and wept by the rivers of Babylon, but now saw in the distance the ancient walls of David's city? To them it seemed at first too good to be true. "We were like them that dream." And yet they knew it was true. "Then was our mouth filled with laughter, and our tongue with singing."

In that pure and beautiful laughter of the returning exiles I hear an echo of the laughter of heaven. We are all exiles in this world. Here we are only pilgrims and strangers, as all our fathers were. We seek and desire a better country; that is, a heavenly one; and we look for another city, a city which has foundations, whose builder and maker is God.

You sometimes hear it said that the Christian Church has placed too much emphasis upon, paid too much attention to, the life to come, and, preoccupied with heaven, has neglected this present life. I do not believe that was ever so. But certainly today the pendulum has swung to the other extreme. Heaven is the neglected territory today. At a meeting of a group of ministers in an Ohio city, the question of sermons on heaven came up, and most of them said that they had never preached a sermon on heaven. But if the devout Jew in captivity needed to have Jerusalem come into his mind, how much more do you and I need to have the "heavenly Jerusalem," the "City of our

God," come into our minds! The Church needs a great revival of faith in immortality and in the heavenly life. The more we neglect the life to come, the poorer we make this present life.

One of the old hymns, speaking of heaven, says, "What joys await us there!" Yes; let Jerusalem come into your mind. Think of the joys that await us there. "Wilt thou shew wonders to the dead?" Yes; God's heaven will show wonders to the dead. First of all, there will be the wonders of meeting and conversing with the notable characters of the Old Testament and the New Testament. Cicero said that he looked forward to conversing with Homer and Hesiod and other heroes of the ancient world. If a pagan could say that, then what about the Christian?

Again, the wonders of heaven will be the wonders of its silence, when we wonder at the revelation of the glorious working out of the providence of God, and see how, in a way we could not except by faith see or understand here, "all things work together for good to them that love God." Also, there will be the wonders of our heavenly activities, for there we shall "go from strength to strength." For the redeemed body, clothed with new and marvelous powers, and the redeemed and purified soul united to the redeemed body, surely there will be tasks and enterprises in keeping with so great a body and a soul. What has Elijah been doing since he went up into heaven in a whirlwind? What has Moses been doing since God buried him in that grave in Nebo's lonely land? What has Paul been doing since the headsman's ax flashed in the sunlight by the pyramid of Caestius outside the walls of Rome and he put on immortality? What have your sainted father and mother been doing since they fell asleep in Christ?

> Somewhere, surely, afar,
> In the sounding labour-house vast
> Of being, is practised that strength,
> Zealous, beneficent, firm!
>
> .   .   .   .
>
> Still thou performest the word
> Of the Spirit in whom thou dost live,
> Prompt, unwearied, as here![3]

Blessed are they that walk by faith here. There they shall walk by sight. Blessed are they that sow in tears here. There they shall reap in joy. Blessed are they that mourn here. There they shall laugh!

[3] Matthew Arnold, "Rugby Chapel."

XVII

"Who hath gathered the wind
in his fists?"

Prov. 30:4

THE FOUR WINDS AND THE
VOICE OF GOD

WE RARELY THINK ABOUT THE WIND EXCEPT ON A COLD winter day when it smites us in the face, or at the end of a close, sultry day when it caresses our check with its soft and cooling breath. What is the wind? Who knows? Where does the wind come from? And when it passes us, where does it go?

All through the Bible you can hear the sound of the wind; sometimes its gentle evening sigh and sometimes the roaring whirlwind. The wind appeared first after the Flood, when God "remembered Noah" and made a wind to pass over the earth—"and the waters assuaged." A mighty wind opened a path through the Red Sea for the children of Israel, and another wind brought the sea back in its might and overwhelmed Pharaoh and his chariots. "Thou didst blow with thy wind, the sea covered them: they sank as lead in the mighty waters." David marched to battle against the Philistines when he heard the sound of the wind, the "sound of a going in the tops of the mulberry trees." It was a great wind from the wilderness which smote the four corners of the house where Job's sons and daughters were eating and drinking, and buried them in its ruins. At the word of the Lord, Ezekiel prophesied unto the wind in the valley of dry bones— "Come from the four winds, O breath, and breathe upon these slain, that they may live. . . . And they stood up upon their feet, an exceeding great army." At the end of our Lord's Sermon on the Mount you can hear the winds blow and beat upon that house which was built on the sand; and it fell, "and great was the fall of it."

On that memorable night when Nicodemus came to see Jesus—perhaps at his favorite resort, the Garden of Gethsemane—as they were talking together the evening wind sprang up. To Nicodemus, perplexed about the mystery of the new birth, Jesus said, Listen, Nicodemus! Do you hear the wind? The work of the Holy Spirit is like that. "The wind bloweth where it listeth, and thou hearest the sound thereof, but canst not tell whence it cometh, and whither it goeth: so is every one that is born of the Spirit."

The winds appear for the last time in the Bible during an interlude in the judgments which fell upon the earth when the seven seals were opened and John saw "four angels standing on the four corners of the earth, holding the four winds of the earth, that the wind should not blow on the earth, nor on the sea, nor on any tree."

Our text is one which you might expect to find in the pages of Isaiah or in the book of Job, with its sublime references to the majesty of God in nature. But, instead of that, we find it amid the maxims and wise sayings of the book of Proverbs. Agur—which may be just another name for Solomon—desiring to contrast the finiteness of man and the infinite power and wisdom of God, asks the question, "Who hath gathered the wind in his fists? . . . what is his name, and what is his son's name, if thou canst tell?" This verse in Proverbs, and one in the book of Revelation about the four angels who are always God's messengers, holding the four winds on the four corners of the earth, speak of the wind as under the authority of God. He "gathers the winds in his fists"; that is, he has power to restrain them and power to loose them.

We take the four winds, then, not in a literal, meteorological sense, but in a figurative sense, as the representatives of God's righteous judgments, his gracious providence in our lives, and the operations of his Holy Spirit on the souls of men. Let us listen to the voice of the four winds.

THE NORTH WIND

We shall speak first to the North Wind. O North Wind, what is thy message? The North Wind answers, "I am the wind of judgment, of retribution, of punishment." The prophets Jeremiah, Isaiah, Ezekiel, and others foretell judgments coming upon Israel, and always they are judgments which come out of the north—from Babylon, or from Assyria, "the rod of God's anger." It was a northeast wind that picked up Paul's ship and hurled it through the sea until it crashed on the rocks of Malta. Modern theology has taken the north wind out of the Bible. There is no Euroclydon of judgment left. Yet God is still a righteous Judge, and he who sows the wind shall reap the whirlwind.

Judgments fall upon nations, as well as upon individuals. General Grant, who fought as a lieutenant through the Mexican War and led the armies of the North in the

Civil War, regarded the latter war with its hundreds of thousands dead as a righteous judgment upon the nation for the unjust war with Mexico, with its sinister purpose to expand the territory of slavery. In his sublime Second Inaugural Address, when the north wind of judgment was still blowing over the nation, Lincoln said, "Fondly do we hope—fervently do we pray—that this mighty scourge of war may speedily pass away. Yet, if God wills that it continue until all the wealth piled by the bondman's two hundred and fifty years of unrequited toil shall be sunk, and until every drop of blood drawn with the lash shall be paid by another drawn with the sword, as was said three thousand years ago, so still it must be said, 'The judgments of the Lord are true and righteous altogether.' "

And what of America today? Eighty years before that judgment of civil strife fell upon the nation, Thomas Jefferson, writing his *Notes on the State of Virginia* on the rock at Harper's Ferry where the Potomac and the Shenandoah mingle their waters, said with a prophet's inspiration, "I tremble when I remember that God is just." We behold this nation of ours planted of the seed corn for which God sifted three kingdoms, and on a continent richly endowed and reserved for it through the ages; a nation with whom God has dealt as with no other people; so greatly blessed with the free Bible, the free church, free schools, free labor, and the Sabbath day—this nation we now behold turning away from God and worshiping the idols of prosperity and power and pleasure, a nation where crime is rampant and where dishonesty and corruption abound in high places and in low places. When we

181

think of this, I wonder if it is time for us too to tremble when we "remember that God is just"?

THE SOUTH WIND

How often the traveler in Bible lands, through Asia Minor, and to the isles of the Aegean Sea, has rejoiced to feel toward sunset, after the heat and glare of the day, the gentle touch of the south wind. Yet the South Wind, which is the most pleasant of all winds, is also the most dangerous of all, for it is the wind of temptation.

Well do I remember the day when, after a long and grueling ride on horseback in fierce Mediterranean heat over the barren mountains of Crete, we came out upon a cliff and looked down on a little landlocked harbor, still called, as it was then, Fair Havens, a crescent of sandy beach protected from the stormy winds. Time ran back for nineteen hundred years, and I saw that great Alexandrian grain ship with its 276 soldiers, passengers, seamen, and prisoners, of whom Paul was one, lying at anchor in that little harbor on the southern shore of Crete, where it had taken refuge from contrary winds. Somewhat farther west along the coast of Crete was the harbor and town of Phenice, a more commodious port with more diversions for the sea-weary crew and passengers. To this harbor the master of the ship planned to sail. But Paul was no novice at sea. He had been shipwrecked three times before this, and "a night and a day had been in the deep," clinging to mast and spar. He warned the centurion, who was in command of the soldiers and prisoners, that the voyage would be one of great danger. But the centurion quite naturally believed the master of the ship rather than this Hebrew prisoner.

At length the contrary wind from the west died down, and the South Wind began to blow softly. Supposing it was now safe to sail, the master gave the order to do so. The anchor was weighed, the vast red mainsail was hoisted; and there she went, like a great crimson bird skimming over the water, and headed for the open sea. But the ship had hardly cleared the promontory to the west when the wind suddenly shifted. The soft South Wind ceased to blow, and a raging wind from the northeast, called Euroclydon, came roaring down from the mountains. All that they could do now was to cut away the tangled gear, pull the lifeboat up on board, undergird the ship with cables to hold her timbers together, throw overboard the cargo of wheat, lower the mainsail, hoist the storm sail, and "let her drive" before the wind and sea. And for fourteen days and nights, when neither sun nor stars could be seen, they "let her drive" through the stormy seas, with prisoners, passengers, and soldiers clinging to broken masts and the sides of the ship, and all hope of being saved abandoned; until at length the ship struck on the rocky cliffs of Malta. That was the end of the great Alexandine grain ship; and had it not been that Paul was on board, and that God wanted him to stand before Caesar, and had given him the lives of all that sailed with him, every one of those 276 persons, officers, soldiers, sailors, and prisoners, would have perished.

What brought that ship to ruin? It was the treacherous South Wind. "When the south wind blew softly," then they set sail. But they soon discovered that the South Wind had only tempted them out of the safe harbor of Fair Havens to let them fall into the hands of the fierce and merciless northeast wind. And therein is a parable of

183

life. Prosperity, riches, ease, earthly pleasures, worldly adulation—all these have their perils.

It is written of one of Judah's greatest kings—in certain respects the greatest of all—Uzziah, great as a ruler, organizer, conqueror, inventor, builder, and agriculturist, that he was "marvellously helped, till he was strong. But when he was strong, his heart was lifted up to his destruction." He transgressed against the Lord his God in going into the temple to burn incense on the altar of incense, and he was smitten with leprosy. Have not our own souls found out that some of the most dangerous periods in our life were when the south wind, the wind of ease, applause, flattery, the favor of man, the pleasures of the body, blew softly? When the South Wind blows softly, remember Paul's shipwreck! Remember Euroclydon!

THE EAST WIND

O East Wind, what is thy message? The east wind answers, "I am the wind of affliction and trial." The East Wind is the most penetrating, the most uncomfortable of all. I can still feel the East Wind blowing in from the German Ocean at Edinburgh on the east coast of Scotland.

Archibald Alexander, the first professor of Princeton Seminary, asked by a student one day if he always had full assurance of salvation, said, "Yes; except when the east wind blows." What he meant was that it is the east wind which awakens and brings to the surface the maladies of the body, and that when that happens, the spirit too is depressed.

By the East Wind God taught Jonah compassion.

Jonah had preached the greatest sermon on record, a sermon that brought a whole city and kingdom to its knees in sackcloth and ashes: "Yet forty days, and Nineveh shall be overthrown." Yet when Nineveh repented and turned from its evil ways, and was not destroyed, Jonah was disappointed and angry. On a hill outside the city he sat down under a booth to see what would happen. Having preached the greatest sermon on record, he now gave expression to one of the greatest definitions of God that we have in the Bible. What he said was: "O Lord, was not this my saying, when I was yet in my country? Therefore I fled before unto Tarshish: for I knew that thou art a gracious God, and merciful, slow to anger, and of great kindness, and repentest thee of the evil."

Then God showed him how true it was that he is a merciful God. The gourd that had shaded Jonah's head was smitten and withered. God sent a "vehement east wind" which beat upon the head of Jonah until he fainted, and in his anger declared that it was better for him to die than to live. But God, who does not deal with us after our iniquities, made use of that east wind to teach Jonah sympathy and compassion. He said to the angry prophet, "Thou hast had pity on the gourd, for the which thou hast not laboured, neither madest it to grow; which came up in a night, and perished in a night: And should not I spare Nineveh, that great city, wherein are more than sixscore thousand persons that cannot discern between their right hand and their left hand?"

In the book of Isaiah there is a verse that through the ages has brought comfort to believing souls—"He stayeth his rough wind in the day of the east wind." These words seem to express the lovingkindness of God, who keeps

185

the rough wind from completing the devastation already wrought by the east wind. Another translation makes it read, "He sigheth with his rough wind," as if to say that God's pity is mingled with his judgment.

The preacher must be careful about personal illustrations, things out of his own life, for the danger is that the much exposed personality of the preacher shall become dull and commonplace. But if the preacher has had a godly mother, one in whose tongue was "the law of kindness"; a mother who, like Dorcas at Joppa, was "full of good works and almsdeeds which she did"; a mother of whom he can say in loving retrospection, "O woman, great is thy faith: be it unto thee even as thou wilt"— if he had such a mother, then he need never hesitate to make use of her to illustrate some proposition or truth in his sermon. Young and old will hear it with delight and with glowing hearts; and perhaps even the angels themselves, out on the balconies of heaven, will put by for a little their melodious harps and listen to what he has to say about his mother.

That is what I propose to do now in speaking of the east wind as the wind of discipline and affliction, and of the blessings which it bestows on the soul. My father, soon after finishing at the theological seminary, went to Scotland to study. That was a rare thing to do, for it was almost a hundred years ago. He was invited to preach in the church at Rothesay on the charming Isle of Bute. When he went into the pulpit, he saw in the pew near him a successful young Scottish cotton manufacturer with his wife, six sons, and two daughters. One of those daughters some years afterwards became his wife, my

186

mother. He brought her from her beautiful home on the outskirts of Glasgow to a little hamlet in Ohio, where he was the minister of the Church of the Covenanters, and established her in the new home he had built on the only hill in all the neighborhood, with the hope that on that hill she might not be so homesick for the hills and glens of her native Scotland. Their firstborn child was named after the mother and the grandmother, Catherine, and was always known as Therina. When she was about three years old, her father and mother took her to Scotland to visit her grandparents. They were so enamored of this beautiful child that they persuaded my mother to leave her with them when she returned to America, with the promise that they would come out to Ohio in the early spring and bring the child with them.

But one day the letter—lest a brief cable should be too shocking—arrived at Northwood, Ohio, with the tidings that Therina was gone. "And there was a darkness over all the earth." I have my mother's diary for those years. After that letter came from Scotland, page after page was left blank—day after day, week after week, month after month. But at length strength came to her equal to her desire, and she found that the grace of Christ was sufficient for her even in this terrible trial. I did not think about it much during the years she was with us; but since she left us, it has often come to my mind how that east wind of affliction brought strength and beauty to her character. Now I understand why it is that when I meet people who knew my mother, they almost always say, "She was a remarkable woman." When I think now of the wonderful interest that she was always able to take in the lives of other people—in their joys, their hopes, and their sorrows—and how those who were in trouble and sorrow came to her and were comforted by her, as Paul puts it, by the comfort wherewith she herself was comforted of God—when I think of this, I begin to understand how that staggering, blighting, terrible sorrow in the death of her first-born child, with the ocean between them, became a fountain of blessing, not only for herself, but for others. Passing through her "valley of Baca," she made it a well of inspiration and comfort for other souls. No; not in vain did the east wind of affliction blow upon her soul.

THE WEST WIND

I had no difficulty in hearing where the North Wind blows in the Bible, and the South Wind, and the East Wind. But what of the West Wind? For a time I listened in vain for the sound of its voice. Then at length I heard it, and in a strange place. When Pharaoh would not let let Israel go, God smote the land with the ten plagues. The eighth of these plagues was the plague of locusts. The East Wind which blew in from the desert brought in a swarm of locusts. So multitudinous were they that they blotted out the light of the sun. The army of locusts devoured the crops and stripped the trees and the vines of every green leaf. They stopped the husbandmen at the plough, the fisherman in the Nile, the laborer in the field, and the priest at the altar. They swarmed into the hut of the peasant, into the temples of Isis and Osiris, and into the palace of Pharaoh—into the kitchen, the banqueting halls, the bedroom.

It was this eighth plague which, more than any other save the last and most terrible of all, the death of the first-born, softened for a little the hard heart of Pharaoh. He called for Moses and Aaron in haste and said: "I have sinned against the Lord your God, and against you. Now therefore forgive, I pray thee, my sin only this once, and intreat the Lord your God, that he may take away from me this death only." Then Moses prayed to the Lord for Pharaoh. And the Lord sent a "mighty strong west wind" which drove away the locusts and buried them in the Red Sea. The terrible plague was lifted. "There remained not one locust in all the coasts of Egypt."

The West Wind is the wind of God's mercy and compassion. It is the wind that blows over every praying and penitent soul. God sends the North Wind of judgment and punishment, and the East Wind of trial and affliction, and he permits the South Wind of temptation to blow upon us. But his favorite wind is the West Wind, the wind of his mercy. Ever he waits to be gracious, for "the love of God is broader than the measure of man's mind." Even to proud, haughty, arrogant, defiant, boasting, blasphemous Pharaoh, when he said, "I have sinned," God sent the west wind of his mercy. And it was only when he hardened his heart again that God loosed on him the North Wind of judgment. "As far as the east is from the west, so far hath he removed our transgressions from us." And who can measure that—the distance of the east from the west?

Listen to the voice of the West Wind as it blows in the Bible. For fifty years Manasseh the King of Judah defied God and filled the land with blood and cruelty and idols; for these crimes he was taken by the Assyrians and mutilated and carried into captivity. But when he repented of his great sin and "sought the Lord," he heard the sound of the West Wind of God's mercy, and it carried him back to Jerusalem and put him again on his throne. When David, after his terrible triple transgression, adultery, murder, and hideous hypocrisy, repented and said, "I have sinned," the prophet Nathan said to him, "The Lord hath put away thy sin." And ever since, David has been telling us of the West Wind of God's mercy and forgiveness. Zacchaeus, who had climbed into the top of that sycamore tree to see Jesus and then made confession of his sin, heard the sound of the West Wind when Jesus said to him—and to you and me—"The Son of man is come to seek and to save that which was lost."

The lost son who came to himself in rags and misery down in the "far country" and said, "I have sinned against heaven, and in thy sight," was carried on the wings of the West Wind back to the house of his father, who saw him when he was yet a great way off, and had compassion and ran and fell on his neck and kissed him, and said: "Bring forth the best robe, and put it on him; and put a ring on his hand, and shoes on his feet: . . . For this my son was dead, and is alive again; he was lost, and is found."

The woman who was taken in adultery, and who lay weeping and fearful at the feet of Jesus, waiting for the first stone to strike her, heard the West Wind blow when there was the sound of the stones falling to the ground from the hands of her conscience-smitten accusers as they went out one by one, and she heard Jesus say, "Woman, where are those thine accusers? . . . Neither do I condemn thee: go, and sin no more." Another woman who was a sinner, and who washed his feet with her tears and dried them with the luxuriant and once wanton hair of her head, felt the gentle touch of the West Wind that night in Simon's banqueting hall when Jesus said to her, "Thy sins are forgiven. . . . Go in peace."

And Peter! O Peter, Peter! If it was thou who denied thy Lord and swore that thou hadst never known him; if, indeed, it was thou, so close to him for three years, so honored by him, and up to that night so true to him— if it was thou, Peter, who did that terrible thing there in the courtyard of the high priest, then I, too, might do it. Yet thou, Peter, even in that dreadful hour felt the West Wind when Jesus turned and looked upon thee. Lord, should I ever do what Peter did, then cast upon me that same divine look! Send to my soul the West Wind of thy mercy and thy pity!

And there was that dying robber, but a little while ago cursing and mocking Jesus on the cross. But when he repented and said to Jesus, "Lord, remember me when thou comest into thy kingdom," immediately the West Wind caught him up and wafted him clear from that blood-stained cross on which he hung into the peace and glory of paradise.

Listen to all the four winds! Heed the North Wind of God's righteous judgments: that the way of the transgressor is hard, and that "the wages of sin is death." Heed the East Wind of God's affliction: that "whom the Lord loveth he chasteneth, and scourgeth every son whom he receiveth," but also that "he stayeth his rough wind in

191

the day of the East Wind." Heed the South Wind of
temptation and danger, for when the South Wind blows
softly, the soul must stay close to its Savior. But above
all, heed the West Wind of God's mercy and pity and
forgiveness: that he waits to be gracious, and that as far
as the east is distant from the west, so far will he remove our transgressions from us, when in repentance and
faith we turn and come unto him.